Young Changemakers

Kristi Maggio

ISBN: 979-8-9874131-2-8 (Hardcover)
979-8-9874131-0-4 (Paperback)
979-8-9874131-1-1 (eBook)

Published by Maggio Multicultural Press

Maggio Multicultural Press books are available at special discounts for bulk purchases. For more information, please contact Kristi Maggio at: kristi@maggiomulticulturalfoundation.org

Book and cover design by Kristi Maggio

Edited and Revised by Kristi Maggio and Arianna Fox

First Edition

DEDICATION

To every young person who feels they need to wait until they get older to start accomplishing their goals and dreams, your time is now! To every adult who clips the wings of youth and wants them to be realistic or conform to the societal "norm," let them fly! Let us not limit the younger generation because of our mistakes or fears, and instead, let us change the future generations by giving them the tools they need to accomplish whatever they set their mind to.

CONTENTS

ACKNOWLEDGMENTS

I would like to thank all the young people who collaborated and worked with me to create this book. Without your stories and your perspectives, without your same mission and vision to help other youth, I would not be able to do this. To Bruce Pulver, thank you for joining me in mentoring and interviewing these young authors and sharing the magic of creating meaning out of their *one word*. To Evan Carmichael, thank you for your support and allowing me to use your story and book "Your One Word," where I got the inspiration to have each of the authors find their one word before writing their chapters. To Glenn Marsden, as always, thank you for your continued friendship and counsel, and sharing your wisdom with everyone who will read this book, as well for your global efforts in mental health awareness through the Imperfectly Perfect Campaign. Finally, to a person who has been both a friend and a mentor to me since the first time we spoke, Naveen Jain, I am forever grateful for your contribution to this book and your inspiration to these young people and everyone that will read it.

Are you a young changemaker?

Want to be a part of the next volume of this series?

Visit young-changemakers.com & tell us your story!

Looking to become an entrepreneur or have gain entrepreneurial skills?

Join our *Introduction to an Entrepreneurial Mindset* course and start believing you can help solve the world's greatest challenges.

Visit maggiovirtualacademy.com/entrepreneur-program

FOREWORD

by Naveen Jain

Intensely Curious Entrepreneur and Philanthropist

What if everything you want is possible?
What if the world can be created exactly as you imagine it?
If you can imagine it, you can create it!

When I wrote, *Moonshots: Creating a World of Abundance*, I shared how curiosity, the most important characteristic a person can have in learning, is diminished over time. We all begin life as a *tabula rasa*, wide-eyed, taking in the world and making sense of it, curiosity unimpeded, imagination unconstrained, creativity unhindered. Then the socialization process begins.

We learn the limits of the world, and our place in it, what we can and cannot do, what we're entitled to, and what we have to fight for. Our institutions, from education to the media, promulgate and reinforce a mindset of pessimism each and every day. The idea of an abundant world where problems can be solved is almost unheard of in popular culture and is replaced with fear and scarcity. The younger generation has been conditioned by society to think of the worst-case scenario, instead of the best-case scenario; to think what if it doesn't work, instead of what if it does work, and the most active and powerful force on this planet, curiosity, is being eradicated from young minds. Our world seems hell-bent on eliminating curiosity all together.

Perceptions acquired in early childhood become the fundamental subconscious "programs" that shape one's character. In other words, our perceptions of the world are downloaded directly into the subconscious – and without any filters. We are literally programmed, and the "programming" I received as a child was no different. One could argue that there was no chance for me to escape the cycle of poverty in India as I was growing up, and I certainly would have had no chance had I continued to think the way I was expected to. Had I followed the rules, I would have never left home.

I would have remained stuck within the bell curve of societal norms and expectations for someone of my "social standing."

Growing up in India according to the "societal rules," there was no chance for me to escape the cycle of poverty that I was born into. However, I had a different idea about how my life could be, and for this type of thinking, I was called a rebel. I was told that I would be disappointed and frustrated and would likely get into trouble. I was actually advised to think smaller! My dad, believing he was protecting me, told me the best I could do would be to become an accountant— that would be the ultimate that I could achieve. Any expectation beyond that would only mean disappointment. Engineering? That was out of the question. That kind of education was not available to poor people. "Why aim so high when you know you're going to fail? You're not meant for that. That's not where you come from." Despite this counsel, I did become an engineer. It turns out that I wasn't any good at it, but that's thankfully not the point! The reason I was considered a rebel was that I didn't follow the rules—*I didn't obey the programming*. My thinking was that if I had followed the rules, I'd still be in India, locked into that same "inescapable" cycle.

I can accept that we acquire many foundational perceptions and beliefs about life long before we've developed a capacity for critical thinking, but I do not accept that these beliefs are in any way permanent, or that we cannot radically alter them at will. No one has to be the victim or slave of their own limiting or sabotaging mindsets or perceptions—or those of others. Whatever has been programmed can be reprogrammed. The human mind is an unimaginably creative and nimble platform capable of defining its reality, infusing perceptions with imagination to generate unlimited possibilities. You could say that my leaving India and becoming an engineer was my first real moonshot. If I could do that, then what else is possible? All it takes is a little imagination—and the right perspective.

The age into which we are born determines our mindset and worldview. If we think about Babyboomers, Generation X, Millennials, and the youngest of the generations, GenZ, we find massive differences in outcomes. GenZ is a fascinating demographic; they're more pragmatic than idealistic. Research conducted by Monster shows that GenZers will do whatever it takes to reach their goals—and entrepreneurship is a major priority, with many starting businesses in high school. Seventy-six percent of GenZers see themselves as the owners of their careers, with nearly half expecting to have their own business. Moreover, two-thirds of them are willing to relocate for a good job and are more than willing to work nights and weekends for a better salary. The GenZer's work ethic also translates to a very different worldview. Research by The Center for Generational Kinetics, for example, shows that 78 percent of GenZers believe the "American Dream" is attainable, which is higher than any other generation. So, in looking at the co-authors of this book who are a part of GenZ, I am not surprised at how they are taking on the world by looking for the solutions to the problems the world faces and believing that they can do something about them at such a young age.

No matter who you are or where you come from, no matter your age, ethnicity, or gender, the right mindset and believing in yourself will make all the difference. I am a real example of this. Mindset is no different than a muscle or a habit. In order for it to become strong and effective, it must be developed and exercised. Like everything, change begins with desire—even a negative desire, like the refusal to accept the existing reality. Once a conscious decision to change is made, you must train yourself to remain focused on your goal. If there is just one defining difference that marks the successful entrepreneur or person in life from the unsuccessful, it is his or her mindset, a determined mindset—a mindset that is prepared to do "whatever it takes."

While many young people are willing to do whatever it takes, it can be difficult for them to understand how to accomplish their dreams or solve real world problems. In my opinion, today's youth have it much easier than when I was growing up because of the ability to connect with anyone and learn anything at the touch of a button. With this being said, I want to share with the readers of this book two important life lessons I taught my children.

When my son Ankur was 10 years old, he told me that one day he was going to make more money than me. I could have said, as many parents probably would say, "Good luck son; I hope you do!"

However, I saw it as a very important teachable moment because there is the misconceived notion in the world that success is measured by the amount of money a person has. So, I sat my son down and said, "I am surprised you think of success as making money. You will never be successful by simply counting the money. Your success will be based on how many lives you will be able to improve. Therefore, if one day you are able to improve more people's lives than I did, I will be so proud of you." My son took that advice, and in college he started Kairos, an organization to help young college students get great mentors like he had when he was growing up. Young people need mentoring to guide their journey to help them live a better life. This lesson taught Ankur to think of success in a different way and helped him focus on helping people more than money. Today he is changing the world by solving problems in affordable housing for young people with his company Bilt.

The second lesson is our daughter, Priyanka. When she was 16 years old, she came to me, and this was the conversation:

Priyanka: "Dad, I know you love science and technology. I want nothing to do with science and technology, so get used to it. I found my true passion, and I'm going to pursue it."

Now, most dads at that time would have said, "Sweetie, I'm so glad you found your passion. I want to help you pursue that passion." However, that was not how I looked at it.

Me: "Sweetheart, you're not letting dad do his job."

Priyanka: "What is dad's job?"

Me: "Dad's job is to expose you to enough things to make the right choices for your life. You're too young to have a passion. You don't even know what you don't know, so how can you possibly tell me you don't like it?"

Priyanka: "What is it that you would like me to do?"

Me: "I want you to go to Singularity University. I want you to learn about nanotechnology, neuroscience, genetics, computer science and artificial intelligence. Then come back and tell me what your true passion is, and then you can pursue it."

Priyanka: "So if I go there, would you promise me that when I come back, I get to do what I want?"

Me: "As long as you go with an open mind, wanting to like and wanting to learn, you have my word."

She went to Singularity University for four weeks, and upon her return:

Priyanka: I made-up my mind.

Me: Honestly, I gave you my word. What is it that you would like to do?

Priyanka: "I've decided I'm going to be either a neuroscientist or geneticist."

Me: "At the risk of you changing your mind, would you tell me what happened?"

Priyanka: "Dad you're so dumb. I'm in high school, and in high school I learn about all this stuff, and I'm thinking why do I care? I look at all this stuff I'm learning and asking myself, what would I ever do with it? When I went to Singularity University, I realized I always cared about women and how I can help them live a better life. If I don't know how their brain works or what genetics is, then I won't know how I can improve their health. So, I realized science and technology are simply the tools in my tool chest for me to do what I want to do."

Since that moment, Priyanka has been using science and technology to make women's lives better. She did exactly what she wanted to do by using the technology to solve that problem, and that to me is the key. Finding something you're passionate about but making sure you get enough "tools in your tool chest," because if you don't and you only have a "hammer," then everything looks like a "nail." You need to explore and experience what is out there that you don't know, so you have a variety of tools. You have "a screwdriver, a wrench, a hammer, a level, etc.," and you can solve multiple problems by using the right technology and by having the right skills to solve the right problem.

Now, perhaps you are unsure of what you can do to make a difference in the world. Perhaps you are allowing fear and the idea of failure to hold you back. Maybe you are uncertain of what your passion or purpose is. If you are young like my children were, that's all right. Learn and experience as much as you can, and you will find it. Also ask yourself important questions and reflect. Simply close your eyes and imagine you have everything you want, and all the money you need. What would you be doing? If you do that, you will get everything you want.

Finally, dream so big that people think you are absolutely crazy! Never be afraid to fail. You only fail when you give up. Ask yourself, "What problem do I want to solve in the world that is so important to me that I would be willing to die for it?"

Now live for it!

INTRODUCTION

Life is an adventure. We don't know what to expect from one day to the next. Sometimes we have ups, and others we have downs. There are challenges and struggles, celebrations, and victories. What makes it an adventure is the unknown. As children, we are guided by our parents or guardians, and we are put on a path of discovery to figure out who we are meant to be. The experiences that we have and the choices that we make become our life, our adventure, no one else's.

Over the past two years I have had the honor of getting to know some extraordinary young adults who are working their way through their personal adventure, and the extraordinary thing about them is that they all have chosen something very different. However, the one thing that remains common among them is their love and passion for what they do, and their desire to make a positive impact on the world around them, especially other young people!

When this book is published, I will have been on my journey for 45 years, and I can truly say it has been an adventure! The choices I made have brought me to where I am today, in creating this book to help other young people find their voice and realize that they too are on this adventure called life. It's not easy. The struggles are real. The challenges are there, but it's how we face them and move forward that ultimately determines the impact that we will have on ourselves and those around us.

You see, it is easy to get caught up in what society thinks we should do with our lives, especially young people. We often hear, "When I get older, I want to write a book. When I get older, I want to be an actor or singer. When I get older, I want to make a difference in the world." Why when you get older? Why not now?

So, this book is meant to show you that you don't have to wait until you get older, you can start now. Today! No longer should we consider youth to be seen and not heard. I have learned so much from the hundreds of young people that I have come into contact with, and they have made me think differently, look at the world differently, and realize, if they can make such a huge impact at a young age, then I can too.

As everyone else has their own story, I struggled as a child. I was overweight for most of my life, made fun of and teased, battled with anorexia and bulimia, faced depression and anxiety, and I had very little self-esteem. Thankfully at that time, social media didn't even exist, because I would have been one of the young people using it to compare myself with others instead of using it to do good in the world. When I look back now and think about many of the choices I made, they could have been very detrimental and had severe consequences because at different moments I gave into peer pressure.

However, I also had incredible experiences; ones that I would never exchange for anything. I was a lifeguard so I could spend summers outdoors. I backpacked through Europe for two months when I was 18. I lived and studied in Italy. I have visited multiple countries; I speak three languages and have two master's degrees. I have a family that loves me very much, even though they didn't always understand my choices. It wasn't until I found a close relationship with God that I started to have more faith in myself and believe that I too could make an impact in the world, and this did not happen until I was 36 years old. Prior to this moment, I played it safe. I got a teaching job, bought a house, had a car, and focused more on what the world told me life should be like, but there was always a burning desire inside of me that felt like something was missing. I knew I was meant for something more, so when I decided to move to the Dominican Republic to perfect my Spanish, this was the moment that I realized something greater was out there for me.

In the past nine years, I was able to find my purpose and be who God made me to be. I started my own school and am creating a system that works for all children. I was able to be my own boss, become an entrepreneur, and work more creatively. I did things I never thought possible like start a radio show and a podcast, interview incredible people and build new relationships, but most importantly help others realize their potential and their gifts at a much younger age.

You see, I wouldn't change anything that happened in my life because all of my experiences were unique to me and got me to the point where I am today. There were multiple setbacks, multiple challenges, but it was how I looked at them, and held on to the faith that I had inside, knowing if I just didn't give up, if I just kept pushing forward and trusting the process, I would accomplish what I set out to do.

I learned that along the way, things don't go as planned. People will try to hold you back; make you think you're dreaming or that you're crazy. However, those people who have created true success in their life did it because they didn't allow the naysayers, or the difficult moments get to them. They persevered and didn't give up.

So, in this book as you read about the different adventures of these young people, I want you to realize that whatever's in your heart today, you can accomplish. This is your life. This is your adventure. Be bold and unstoppable, as you are the "star" in the role of your life!

CHAPTER 1

Inspire

Young Changemakers

#INSPIRE
Arianna's One Word

I- Initiate the conversation

N- Notice other people's interests

S- Speak with power and confidence

P- Positively influence your peers

I- Illustrate your peers' struggles using inspiring stories

R- Reach out to people in need

E- Empower others to succeed

Young Changemakers

THE TREK TO SUCCESS

"You Rock, Dream Big, and You Got This!"—*Arianna Fox*

Entrepreneur, Best-Selling Author, Keynote Speaker, Actress, Voiceover Talent, and Teen Influencer

All the best stories start with "once upon a time," don't they?

So, climb upon a comfortable couch and get ready for the story of a young girl who had always thought she had to wait until she was older to achieve her dreams. This story contains twists and turns, good and bad scenarios, as well as successes and failures.

This is the story of my trek to success.

Once upon a time, a young four-year-old girl (AKA me) was moving around near the fireplace, keeping her—er, my—constantly hyper self very active with a few dances as my parents sat on the nearby couch. Then, I stopped: A massive revelation had hit me, and I had to *immediately* tell my parents.

I went up to them and said with a look of dead seriousness and a tone of voice equivalent to that of Minnie Mouse, "I want to be an *author* when I grow up."

Do you see what's wrong with this picture? I'll give you a hint: the last four words.

Upon my saying this, my parents immediately supported my decision and were excited to hear that I was so determined, but they asked one important question before further discussion: ***"Why wait? Why not start now? Why wait until you're an adult to achieve your success?"***

And at four years old, my tiny little mind was blown.

Now, at sixteen, I am a girl entrepreneur, Amazon best-selling and triple author, motivational speaker, actress, voiceover talent, and teen influencer. I have been blessed to have done voiceover work for brands such as Amazon, Edible Arrangements, Taco Bell, Plato's Closet, Marriott Hotel, St. Jude's Children's Hospital, Sky Zone, and Old Navy. However, my mission is simple: to inspire, energize, and uplift others—particularly youth—in any way I can. One of the aforementioned ways I like to inspire and uplift people is through the intricate and complicated world of **social media.**

It is an oft disputed topic, as some people say that social media is a brilliant invention and nearly live by, while others claim that it is harmful to teenagers and should not be used. I think that both claims are somewhat right; at least, they both contain true aspects. Social media is indeed a brilliant invention, and yes, it does possess the ability to be harmful—especially to teenagers, who are practically more conscious about their self-image than people of any other age. It is also true that there is so much negativity on social media these days. However, social media is also a platform to spread inspiration and positivity, if that is what *we* choose to spread. Social media, in many ways, is what *we* make it. Thus, I choose to make it positive, entertaining, and educational.

I have often pleasantly surprised people when I told them that I like to put up educational quizzes on my Instagram stories for my followers, and I make them fun with vivid colors and catchy wording. Among many other things, I've put up quizzes on unique educational subjects such as synesthesia (a perceptual phenomenon in which certain senses are blended together), the true origin of the Mexican holiday Cinco de Mayo, and even how to properly pronounce seemingly difficult Irish names (like Siobhán or Éabha).

I once told someone, "I want my followers to log off Instagram one day and think, 'Wow, I learned something new and cool from Arianna today!' That is one of many things that social media can be good for: teaching and learning new things! I wish for social media to be useful, positive, and practical, not just full of addicting entertainment that does nothing for the brain *or* the soul. I wish to spread—and hopefully to see more people spreading—messages that most teenagers don't see online today. I wish to spread messages of hope, inspiration, and self-confidence—messages of working hard, staying true to yourself, and never giving up.

Speaking of giving up, I want to share a pivotal moment in my life that I'll never forget, the likes of which you may have or may be experiencing right now…at this very moment.

Ever since I was young, I've always loved acting. I wasn't a professional actress at the time I began to love it, mind you, but I adored it nonetheless. To adopt the mind of another character—

especially one which I created—was freeing and invigorating. (It still is!) It all started with what we called "Production," in which I would run around the room like a maniac and pretend to be different created characters. It was fun. (And yes, it still is.)

However, it was only recently at approximately the age of thirteen when I began, with the help and support of my parents, to really take acting seriously. I entered the increasingly confusing world of the entertainment industry and began performing auditions, landing myself in a few movies, shorts, and series here and there. I wasn't too bad at memorizing and most of the time, my auditions went all right, but then, things started to go south. Auditions became increasingly difficult, and I was having the hardest time memorizing my lines.

Finally, the last straw broke the camel's back. I had a virtual Zoom audition for a well-known talent agency. This was one of the easiest auditions of all time; it consisted of a simple mock commercial monologue for Kraft Macaroni and Cheese. *I'll rock this*, I told myself confidently, and I memorized the script to what I thought was the best of my ability. Then, later that evening, it was time to enter the virtual meeting room. I realized I wasn't the only one in the meeting, and that people were performing in front of the talent agents, *and* all the rest of the kids who were waiting to audition—but no matter; I wasn't nervous at all. When was I ever? I waited as name after name was called, and kid after kid entered and performed various monologues. Finally, my name was called—just like the others—in the most dull, exasperated monotone that ever I heard.

"Tell us your name, age, and a little about yourself," the agent instructed.

I gladly did so.

"Okay, now go ahead with your audition."

I nodded. "Here I go…."

I opened my mouth, expecting words to come out—but they didn't. My thoughts, in a sense, were blocked as if a dam had suddenly been placed over a mental waterfall. I went completely blank.

Trying not to panic, I requested a chance to start over again. They gave it to me whilst side-eyeing each other in their virtual Zoom boxes and saying, "Please note that this is Arianna's *second* take."

Finally, I thought I had it. I got a few words out…and then I blanked out once again. No words emerged victoriously from the mental block like I expected them to. My mind was as a white sheet of paper.

That was it; there were no more second chances. I left the Zoom meeting, my heart full of regret, frustration, and disappointment. Why had this happened? Why wasn't I ready? Why didn't I succeed? I was crestfallen with a whirlwind of emotions.

A few weeks later, I contemplated giving up on acting in general. I wasn't feeling it. There was very little passion left, and I thought perhaps I could focus on other endeavors. However, my parents taught me something very important: **I was using my past to determine my future.** I was focusing too much on what *happened* as opposed to what *could* happen if I didn't give up, and I pushed through. Just because I momentarily didn't have much passion, that didn't mean that it wasn't my purpose. With the help of my parents, I learned the valuable lesson of not giving up, and that is one of the most important things I want you to glean from this story of mine. You see, we make mistakes all the time—in fact, it's a part of life and the learning process—but the vital thing to do is learn from them and keep going. You don't fail if you make mistakes. **You only fail if you give up.**

So, in conclusion, I hope to spread this very message to more people through speaking events, books, and any other way that I can continue to empower others. That is my ultimate goal and vision for the future: to spread more positivity in this world that is currently all too overpowered by negativity—to inspire.

Quotes I live by:

"We breathe. We pulse. We regenerate. Our hearts beat; our minds create; our souls ingest. Thirty-seven seconds well used is a lifetime."—Mr. Magorium, *"Mr. Magorium's Wonder Emporium"*

"Education never ends, Watson. It is a series of lessons with the greatest for the last."—Sherlock Holmes

"You Rock, Dream Big, and You Got This!"—Arianna Fox

My one word is Inspire.

That very word — "inspire"— carries much more weight to me than you might think. It sums up my ultimate goal and life purpose. To inspire others and to change lives can be so rewarding, and it makes us feel fantastic. However, I consider myself something of a practical person, and I recognize that not everyone automatically knows "how to inspire others." Thus, I made an acrostic to sum up some of the steps to making a greater impact upon the lives of your peers. These may seem like small tasks, but trust me, the small steps are so incredibly vital. As my favorite fictional character, Sherlock Holmes, once said, *"The little things are infinitely the most important."*

The truth is, whether you are a young person who wants to be an entrepreneur, an author, an artist, a musician, or practically *any* career path you wish to choose, it is all up to you when you decide to take action. When people ask me how I find motivation, I tell them I don't search for it; I *create* it. So, whatever your passion is—whatever it is that you love, that you enjoy doing, even if it feels more like work than fun sometimes—don't wait for adulthood or inspiration but pursue it with all your heart; and above all, *never give up.*

CHAPTER 2

#CONSISTENT
Riyad's One Word

C - Confidence in Uprising

O - Overcoming the Fears

N - Name every dream of yours and make it true

S - Strengthening the Weaknesses

I - Igniting the Inner Self

S - Sail Through Success

T - To tackle the waves of agitation and terror and rise up

E - Enormous is an elephant, and so is dreaming to achieve

N - Nest the positive thoughts and the negative ones fly away

T - Talent in us can be approved by the public only if we let our minds to do so

Young Changemakers

I (DREAM + THINK + ACHIEVE)

"Every mind is a discovery of its own kind." - Riyad Maroof Hassan

Author, Entrepreneur, Director,
Talk Show Host, Child Rights Advocate

I am keen to expand the power of the mind to every point in the world and am dedicated until I stop breathing. Every human present on this earth belongs to a generation, and everyone was once or is a part of the youth society. This society is renowned to be the society with stairs to the future. I, being a part of it at the present time, aim to contribute as much as I can to help construct the stairs. I have been successful in sharing my ideas in nearly 100 international conferences, student exchanges, summits, events, meetups, and many more, in a span of two years. I believe that sharing an idea is better than knowing it, and I do the same as well. I have established a one-of-a-kind child council, a media production to educate through entertainment, and an ed-tech startup to develop every form of creative education to every door. As an author, I write in magazines and periodicals to symbolize what the youth can do and what makes them the uprising.

Social media plays a vital role in shaping a person who aspires to be renowned. You would find a 90-year-old man and a 10-year-old boy as its users, and nothing seems strange here. My eyes caught this game-changer when I was 11 years old. Facebook was the most downloaded and famous social networking application during our childhood. One year passed post my debut book publication, and I wanted to expand my readers. I created a page on Facebook which helped me achieve my dream and I named it 'Literature on Screen.' I received a positive response from the readers and was successful to gain nearly a thousand people in a year. That marked the beginning, but the journey was way different. I lost consistency the next year and stopped it temporarily. In 2020, the pandemic let me start something new again. It was the time when my media house, *The Clippers TV*, was born from a small interview I conducted. Two years have passed by, and we have a network of more than 10, 000 people in around 15+ countries and 100+ cities. Through this wonder, my dream goal of making the world a better place to live in is turning into a fact. I believe this entire idea of social media depends on its usage. Next time, when someone distinguishes you from social media by your age, tell them, "It's not the AGE that matters, it's the USage that does."

There was a time, and there is always, which you would like to remember, even if it brings you laughter or tears. I penned my first story when I was 5 years old, but it was discontinued until I wrote the next one when I was 8. I received rejection and no one knew that it would be my roller coaster ride for today.

I once used to hate grammar and the errors awaiting my exams. My 3rd Standard English scores were not that good and the assigned teacher complained to my parents. They had a punishment for me in mind. I was given a pen in my right hand, and a piece of paper in my left. The task was to write two paragraphs on two subjects but the hardest one arrived a little later. It was story writing that was chewing my mind. I took a nap and suddenly moved into a dream. I was a sailor and the tale continued till it had a happy ending. I woke up and found it! I now knew how to write a story! That day, I understood that anything in literature that makes sense and has a flow of our imagination can be a story.

I read it to another teacher in excitement, and she connected me to the newspaper office where her husband works. She also promised to put it on the school's literary wall. With loads of joyfulness, I entered the office and submitted it to him. It was four weeks now, and I had no response. Later on I got to know that they judged my age without reading my story. Unfortunately, my story was not even on the wall. I stood stubborn. Ideas popped into my mind and I kept on writing.

Two years passed and my debut book was published at the age of 10, and consecutively, the next year, I received the Youngest Writer of Assam award. People were congratulating me and in between, a message popped in. I was in the headlines of that same newspaper that rejected my story. It was not a huge milestone, but it was a milestone. It played a vital role in shaping me. Hence, I dream, I think, and I achieve. I take it as my motto for the next decades I wish to live in and work on.

The greatest possible vision for the future I have is to unite every single person with the power of love, harmony, education, culture, and respect. I dream of forming a place where a faithful man gains the highest account of knowledge.

Quotes I live by:

"The true sign of intelligence is not knowledge but imagination."
- Albert Einstein

"Every mind is a discovery of its own kind." - Riyad Maroof Hassan

CHAPTER 3

#HOPE

Kellina's One Word

H- Having no control over many situations but making the best out of every one

O- Open-mindedness is crucial; do not allow anybody to define who you are. You can be yourself.

P- Patience is key to a successful life.

E- Everything happens for a reason; don't be hard on yourself.

EVERY DAY I AM JUST DEAF

Kellina Powell

Entrepreneur, Advocate for the Deaf Community, Public Speaker, Author

My mission is to bridge the gap between the deaf and hearing community. I want the deaf community to feel involved within the hearing community. As an advocate and coach for the hard of hearing community, I realize it is not easy to be part of the community where you don't fit. As a young person who is able to communicate in two different groups, I am able to show the lack of education there is on this topic in different communities. I have learned that there are limits to education that should be taught. This is where my mission comes into the picture, I want to show people that it is okay to feel different.

Spreading awareness is key, and I am doing this by attending networking events, speaking on podcasts, and presenting at public speaking events. This allows me to meet different people around the globe. Since podcasts are getting popular, a lot of people are starting to listen to them more than radio. Ever since I became aware of my audience, I began meeting people to collaborate on various projects.

While social media is both beneficial and detrimental, it has allowed me to connect within my community outside of my country. Social media can be used for business or personal use, as well as keeping in touch with lost friends or family. I never thought social media would direct me to my career path being an influencer, author, and speaker. I was able to gain more knowledge and learn habits very quickly, as well as expand my audience with other communities, not just the deaf community. I am grateful to meet all the new people that are impacting my life, and I am starting to realize that technology is the new generation, as I never thought I would be meeting my business friends through Clubhouse, Instagram, or Facebook. I understand that social media has a negative impact on different people, however, people need to be aware of how they are spending time on social media, what they are feeding their brain and using it to make positive impact in the world.

We all face important pivotal moments that shape our lives. I was working at a park called Canada's Wonderland and during my break, a little boy approached me and said, "Miss, miss look." (While he was pointing to his hearing aid) I looked very shocked, and I said wow. I had a small conversation with the little boy, and his mom approached me proudly and said, "Wow you made a change in my son's life by simply showing your hearing aid and putting your hair back." The mom said something that made me have a second thought about my career. She said, "You will make an impact and change the world just by doing simple things." It will always sit with me forever because I have never once had someone come up to me and say that. So, what we might think is trivial or unimportant, can have a lasting impact on someone who really needs it.

My vision for the future is to expand my business globally and educate people about the deaf community. I want to change the movie industry by making movies more accessible to the hard of hearing and have more representation among those with disabilities. I would love to meet Tyler Perry and make a movie with him. Lastly, I would like to write dozens of books for children and adults to connect both sides and come together to not judge one another.

CHAPTER 4

ENCOURAGE

Be a Light In Darkness
& See The
Compounding Effects

#ENCOURAGE
Zackary's One Word

E- Educate and empower others

N- Notice what needs to be done and finish what you started

C- Connect and get to know people for who they are and reach out to people often

O- Optimism will light up a room and the people around you

U- Uplift others everywhere you go and have unity in your community

R- Reassure, be empathetic, and communicate with others

A -Accountability and integrity will help build trust and confidence in yourself and others

G- Give to others and support their needs, always being a good-natured and kind person

E- Engage and include others in group activities and conversations

THE JOURNEY TO TRANSFORMATION

"Get Up, Get Moving, and Live an Inspired Life" —*Zackary Ford*

Content Creator, Podcaster, Independent Christian
Singer/Rapper/Songwriter/Musician,
Aspiring Author, Motivational Speaker, and Teen Influencer

What is the adventure of life without a journey to walk through? Sit back in your comfortable chair or the warm blankets on your bed and get ready to hear the story of a young man who felt the pressure to be his best, but sometimes fell short of his expectations and over-thought every situation. Then soon transforming his perspective from a fixed mindset to a high-potential, problem-solving, innovative spirit full of curiosity. This story takes you back to who I was as a young kid and through a journey of how I changed and developed myself over the years until today and who I'm working to become.

When I was a young little munchkin learning what I enjoyed doing, I found joy in expressing my ambitious personality and fun, crazy, energetic spirit. The only thing that blocked me when I was younger, was that I was shy and introverted in public around people that were triple my size it seemed. Whenever my parents took us, the kids, to the grocery store or other public places and events, I stood directly walking behind my parents holding tightly as if I was to never let go.

However, as I got older into my young teenage years until today, I've grown immensely out of my shell, from practically despising interacting with unfamiliar people, to walking up to random people in school and public to introduce myself and spread love and encouragement. I definitely bubbled up and developed an extroverted personality, and my life has forever transformed and led to me working on my personal development, dreams, goals, and unwrapping my gift inside to present to the world.

I've developed a spirit of confidence, courage, and a determination to make an impact on others through the gifts, stories, and unique life God has given me. I am indefinitely and forever grateful for the life I have and who I'm becoming every day. From a shy young soul to an outgoing person, who has the drive to transform and positively impact the lives of many people through my creative work endeavors, I am taking life day by day to see where this journey takes me.

Waking up every morning knowing God has given me another day to live, I know I have a purpose and destiny that still needs to be fulfilled. We get "one life" that's it. What we do every day impacts our tomorrow and following actions. Therefore, to transform your life, the work and decision start TODAY, not tomorrow or next week, but this very day, this very moment you are living. Now that I'm sixteen, I am a digital creator, songwriter, music artist, podcaster, and aspiring author writing my first book. I consider myself a teen influencer working to change the lives of many people. I am blessed to have the opportunities I have, so I must utilize my skills, ideas, resources, environment, and work ethic to help others. My mission, however, is simply to encourage, empower, and educate the youth and all generations of this world, in any way possible, no matter what it takes to achieve this reality.

Social media has its pros and cons and people have differing opinions and beliefs about the effects on a person's brain and lifestyle. Social media can be very valuable when you are building an audience and want to impact and influence your audience. People see you for how you live your life, what you say and what you do, your characteristics and integrity, and who you present yourself to be. However, what we post online isn't always the truth or at least a mostly filtered version of the truth and our real lives and experiences.

Life is hard sometimes, however, we as people and society don't typically share the dark or vulnerable moments and situations we each face. We share the good moments and present our "highlight reel" to our friends and followers online. Don't get me wrong, this is not necessarily a bad or wrong thing to do. Rather, the important thing to realize is that we have the choice of what we share on social media, plus what we allow ourselves to consume, follow, and believe.

Social media has its bad and addicting sides, however, depending on how we consume and use social media, is truly what matters and has an effect on our experience with it and how we allow it to impact our lives. There are many good qualities of social media I've noticed, such as having the opportunity to encourage and educate people in various ways, also the chance to inspire, teach and provide resources for people to grow their skills and knowledge in different ways.

People have many pivotal moments that shape their lives. For me, I have seen sports as pivotal and immense part of people's lives, myself included. I played soccer for a few seasons, about 3-5 years, when I was in elementary school, with Coach Deshan (I believe that was his name). A critical part of this story comes with a very important life lesson I learned. When I was on the sidelines waiting to play in the games we had, instead of focusing on the game and players, many times I was purposely distracted and off-task. I was causing not only myself but some other players sitting on the sidelines on my team to be distracted too with eating snacks we had available. I learned a very important life lesson about how when I was being distracted, this caused my coach to see me as not caring about and valuing the game or my fellow teammates as I should've. Therefore, he didn't give me barely any playing time on the field in the games because he saw I didn't value myself enough to focus on the game and be a quality team player with good sportsmanship.

I remember one game we had; I only played about 15 minutes in the 4th quarter for the whole game because of how my coach saw me when I was in practice and on the sidelines during games. The lesson represents when you are unfocused, distracted, and not intentional with what you're doing, you will lose out on potential opportunities (in my case -- losing out on playing time on the field). This is a reminder to get focused and not allow yourself and the people around you to get you off track of your goals and lead you away from "what's important" in your life.

There's the concept of the 5 people you hang around most is who you become, and if you are distracted and not goal-focused, you are showing others that you don't have respect for yourself and in a way, don't value yourself enough to work towards your goals and dreams. You also influence and show others that not working toward your goals and living a care-free distracted life is okay. It's NOT! You have value, importance, and potential, and you can choose to leave your gifts and talents wrapped up inside or let them out to the world.

Something I've heard and learned from an interview on Tom Bilyeu's Podcast with Trent Shelton was when Trent said something very valuable that will transform your perspective. He said in the interview, "...you're doing the world a disservice by leaving your gift wrapped up. Somebody needs your story. My mom told me this, and I'll never forget it." She said Trent, "You're assigned to reach people. I don't know how many, but you're assigned to reach people that nobody else can reach but you. Everybody has that, and the more you leave your gift wrapped, those people that need your message, that need your encouragement, whatever it is, that need your talent, they're never going to get it, and you're not going to leave this world a better place."

This interview and message from Trent reminded me of the value of life, the choices we make every day and who we choose to be. Plus, what we do every day impacts every other decision we'll make and our future life. Knowing that YOU, the individual, are the main reason and changemaker for the life you have, this realization will alter the daily decisions you decide to make. Also, every day they'll slowly compound upon one another and create the present reality you have at this moment. Therefore, having self-awareness of the actions, thoughts, and beliefs you hold will lead to more opportunities you can take on.

In closure, I envision spreading encouragement and life-changing inspirational messages through social media content, music, songwriting, books, speaking engagements, interviews, networking, and any way to uplift others. I want to be a light by empowering people's lives and lead them to know who they are and recognize their value and potential. I aspire to empower several millions of people to know their purpose, gifts, and talents. Plus, I will help individuals understand that their personal stories and experiences matter and need to be shared with the world. Everyone has a voice and people to impact, and world change begins with each person impacting their community. Someone needs to hear your voice and life story.

Quotes I live by…

Don't judge each day by the harvest you reap but by the seeds that you plant.
-Robert Louis Stevenson

"If you look at what you have in life, you'll always have more. If you look at what you don't have in life, you'll never have enough." -Oprah Winfrey

"Get Up, Get Moving, and Live an Inspired Life" —Zackary Ford

My one word is Encourage.

This word —encourage— holds much more value and importance to me than you might believe. Having this characteristic is a valuable and empowering skill and virtue to have because this emphasizes how words of encouragement can have a huge impact on people's lives. Words and actions can destroy or uplift an individual's whole persona and influence their life. Therefore, having the trait of encouragement resembles how to transform not only your own life but also the lives of many others through your words and actions. Therefore, my acrostic in the beginning of this chapter shows the process and steps of how to use encouragement in your everyday life to transform others' lives one day, one story, and one interaction at a time.

CHAPTER 5

"I WISH I KNEW THEN…"

By Evan Carmichael

Serial Entrepreneur, International Speaker,
Author, Venture Capitalist

In this book, you will notice that all the Young Changemakers have a # with their "one word." They all went through the process I laid out in my first published book called, *Your One Word*. It is the word that defines a person, their mission, and their purpose. My one word is #believe. I have been built to serve entrepreneurs and help other people believe in themselves. I think it is equally important that youth start believing in themselves now, which is a much younger age than I did. So, why is my one word *believe*? Let me explain…

From the moment you were born, you were told who you had to be. You were told what to eat, what to wear, and what school to go to. You were told what job you should take, by what age you should be married, how many kids you should have, and what someone like you is "supposed" to do. No one ever really asks you what you want, what your dreams are or what makes you happy. You might even be afraid to share those thoughts because of what people around you might say. Maybe you even shared them and were told to be more "realistic." The reason most young people have a hard time believing in themselves is because the world around them isn't exactly being supportive or believing in them either.

As a child, I always seemed to be a slow learner. When I went to school at 3, I spent a lot of time sitting under my desk instead of participating in class. Around the age of 8, my mom began to notice some serious changes in me as I went from being a happy child, adventurous and curious, to becoming more withdrawn and developing nervous ticks. I never did well in school, never really had many friends, and my teachers always accused me of just doing the bare minimum and not trying.

I was always grateful to my parents for their support because they always said, "You are Evan Castrilli Carmichael and you can do anything you believe you can." As well, I was always grateful to my mentor in grade 12, Mrs. Farr, as she was the first outside my family to help me believe in my potential. It turned out that I wasn't stupid at all; I just needed a little extra help. In my last year of high school, I went from getting B's and C's to getting an A+ in every class and a full scholarship to the university of my choice.

Let me stop here for a moment, because if you are at all going through what I went through at this very moment, I want you to realize it's not your fault, and I understand exactly how you feel. Now is the time to start believing in who you are and what you are capable of. It's time to start ignoring anyone or anything that is holding you back. It's a big step, but you can do it!

Now let's continue to the next stage… university. When I graduated high school, I thought I had it all figured out; go to university, study economics, and become an investment banker. However, when I got to university, I got the opportunity to join two entrepreneurs who had started a software company, and they offered me a 30% stake in the business to join them. The more I worked on my new business, the more I realized that nothing I was learning in my university economics classes was helping me.

So, at 19, I had to make the hardest decision of my life: stay with the company I owned where I was only making $300 per month or take the six-figure investment banking job I dreamed of. I struggled a lot with the decision and my mind was going through all the negative thoughts like, *"What if I'm not good enough to be an entrepreneur? What if I don't make it? What if I can never support myself? What if I blow my one chance to make it as an investment banker? Can I really turn down six figures when I'm only making $300 per month? What will people say if I turn this job of a lifetime down?"* Sound familiar? Isn't it funny how we automatically tend to think about what if it doesn't work instead of what if it does?

At this point, I decided that I'd take a year off and invest in myself instead by trying to make my business work. I was inspired by Amazon founder Jeff Bezos, who left his high-paying investment banking job to become an entrepreneur because he didn't want to live with the regret of not knowing. So, I decided that **I didn't want to have regrets** when I was older; I would rather know and fail than regret it later. I turned down the job and went to work full time on my business. You don't know until you actually try, so I went for it!

I was working all day, every day on my business, but nothing seemed to be working. No matter how much I tried, how long I worked, how many ideas I came up with, none of them had an impact. I couldn't believe it and went back to feeling like the dummy I was for most of my school life. I made it harder on myself because I didn't tell anyone I was struggling. I was embarrassed and ashamed that I wasn't having success. I told my friends that I couldn't go out with them because I was "hustling" and "living the entrepreneur life," but really, I was just broke and felt like a loser. So, after having this feeling of being a worthless failure building and building inside me, I called my business partner and said, "I quit. I need to feel like I have some kind of value as a human and this business of ours is not working."

Can you believe it? I quit but… not for long. I realized I didn't try everything yet, and if I didn't try everything, then I would regret it! Knowing I couldn't go on like this, I had to find another way to win, and here is where it all changed, by asking myself one simple question! Since my business was a software company, I asked myself, "Who has built a successful software company before?" The first person I thought of was Bill Gates from Microsoft. I studied how he built Microsoft from zero and applied that to my business. Shortly after, I got my first deal for $13,500. I couldn't believe it! That may not sound like a lot of money to you, but it was more money than I had ever seen in my life and, more importantly, I had a system I could follow to get more deals. I wasn't worthless! I just needed the right model to follow. Once all of this came to me, I understood much better what I needed to do, but then I learned another hard lesson. I lost a $40 million dollar deal because of my perfectionism!

I'm afraid of making a mistake, getting it wrong, and embarrassing myself. (Perhaps you struggle with the same feelings. Have you ever felt this way?) While it is good to be prepared, nothing can ever be perfect. So, in planning to expand the business and make us millions, I worked and worked on the plan. However, when I was almost done, I second-guessed yet another thing I had in it, so I worked on it some more. FINALLY, I decided that it was perfect. It was done. It was exactly what I wanted and so we took it to market. Our bold new plan to get our business acquired and make us rich was ready! The big idea was to have a giant company in a competing industry buy us. After hearing 'no' multiple times of what I thought was perfection, a big company did really want our product. However, they didn't buy it. Why might you ask? Because they kept with the company they had already spent a lot of time talking to, and they wanted to move quickly. They ended up paying $40 million for our rival company, and immediately I realized, had I not been so much of a perfectionist, we could have gotten to them sooner.

So, in sharing to the younger generation reading this book, I will sum up the key lessons from these stories of what "I wish I knew then…"

1. Your confusion, lack of self-confidence, and lack of belief are not your fault; however, you must do something today that will help you overcome and make you realize that you are worthy of your dreams and that you have great potential.

2. Find the right people to support you and mentor you. My mentor in high school changed my life. She believed in me which made me start believing in myself.

3. When you go to make a decision in your life, get rid of the ANTs (any negative thoughts) and think about what if I do succeed, what if it does work, instead of what if it doesn't.

4. Make sure you give your everything to what you are working on before giving up. It doesn't matter what it is, just make sure you have tried everything possible. If not, you will regret it later in life and always wonder what could have happened had you just stuck with it.

5. Look to those who have succeeded in what you want to do and imitate their model. There is nothing wrong with looking at those who are more successful in your space and learning from their journey and how they did it.

6. Value progress over perfection. As you heard with the company and missing out on the sale, nothing will ever be perfect. Something will always need to be fixed or changed. Even with my YouTube channel, I wanted perfection and never got very far. It took me 4 years to realize this, and it wasn't until I found my mentor who knew what he was doing that I finally started letting go of perfection and focusing on progress. You will suck in the beginning, and THAT'S OK, I did too. If you don't believe me, then check out my first videos on my channel. You will get a good laugh!

7. Mentors are not just important for youth, but they are just as important as you become an adult. Depending on your goals, always find someone who has done what you are looking to do and reach out for their help. People who don't understand what you are doing, won't support what you are doing. So, find those who believe in you, and the day will come when you believe in yourself.

CHAPTER 6

Young Changemakers

#MOTIVATED

Noor's One Word

M- Maturely think of actions and their consequences

O- Open yourself to new challenges and experiences

T- Think before making decisions, yet don't overthink them. Sometimes all we need is to experience them

I- Inspire others and aspire to be great

V- Value the good and bad moments

A- Ambition is always the key for success

T- Try! You never know what God has for you

E- Entrepreneurship or education, we can all choose our own "E" as both fit in terms of success

D- Driven is the explanation to why we do what we do; what we're driven by differs but in the end that's what we're about

I'M NOT JUST A GIRL

My vision of the future is a world where helping each other is the norm… not a good deed. – Noor Yousef Aldalahma

Tech Freak, Sports Addict, and Coach

My mission is to use the power of technology to make this world a better place, to make disabled people live the same way we live, and to make our lives easier through technology. I've always seen people around me struggling in doing daily activities and wished I could've helped. Starting with my great grandma, who once fell and broke her hip, where no one was with her which led to different consequences and led to her death. I started the idea of a fall detector bracelet which indicates when a person falls and sends messages to her caregiver and family and then calls emergency. It was my way of grieving. Then comes the blind project, in which we invented a system that helps blind people in universities live normal lives and helps them know how to move between colleges through their phones and systems connected throughout the university. I want to make our environment a better place too, and that's where I started working on filtering water through fast food waste. You know fast food waste, the major waste found in USA dumps, was used to make drinkable water through filtering contaminated water. That's my mission, making the world a better place through tech.

I have won a couple of awards through my journey, a silver medal in genius Olympiad, best robot design in the Arab region in the Arab robotics championship as well as silver medal in the ELO (Arab region).

Social media has impacted my entire journey. It has allowed me to connect with people of different mindsets and different cultures, as well as play a huge role in learning robotics. The fact that I was able to take so many courses in robotics through just the internet is incredible. Learning through social media is probably not what people use social media for, however in my opinion, that's how it can be used best. Clubhouse through Covid was the place where I learned and heard stories of billionaires talking about success. It was my space to fill my time, and it's the place where I realized that learning through the internet is the best place for a person to get information as well as learn how to communicate and socialize in different languages and with different cultures.

Individual moments shape who we are, so in telling a pivotal one, can be difficult. So, where do I even start! Covid was probably the most pivotal time. I was very engaged in sports at the time. I was a second-degree black belt holder; I played soccer; I coached basketball, so sports were a major part of my life coming from a family who idolizes sports. Covid came after I had a major sports injury in which I wasn't even allowed to go up the stairs. It came right when the doctor told me I wouldn't be able to play sports ever again in my life. It was when I was told my dreams in sports were gone because no matter what, my body couldn't climb our house stairs. Then when covid hit, I was between four walls trying to do anything, just anything.

I remembered joining Quran online classes, where we memorized the Quran and some other religious stuff when my friend asked me to join the online course of a robotics club. I agreed and that was a game changer. It all started from there, and while many struggled through this time, it was my happy time.

There were a lot of moments that shaped me. Moving between countries and changing lots of schools got me adapted to change. So, when Covid hit I already knew I had to find an escape just like when I changed countries or when I moved between 5 schools in 8 years. However, let me be clear, even after all of that, I'm not a fan of constant change. I found that me being busy is my way of coping with stress, anxiety, and over thinking. My way has always been keeping myself busy, and through Covid, solving Rubik's cubes and making robots was my way. That was the start of it, and then after Covid, when I started to go to an in-person academy for robotics. My robotics coach played a huge role in making me brainstorm my ideas and bringing them into existence. He's the reason my journey in robotics is still going. He never told me I couldn't do something, he used to stay up late with me to do my projects. They were puzzle pieces that just got into their right places that made everything possible.

My vision of the future is a world where no one feels there is anything that is impossible. Where through tech, the paralyzed can feel the joy of walking, the blind can enjoy seeing, idolizing nature, and having peace. A world where helping each other is the norm… not a good deed.

Quotes I live by:

"You may hate a thing although it is good for you and may love a thing although it is evil for you. Allah knows, and you do not." ~ Quran

"Don't live life without a purpose, rather, make an impact and leave behind a good memory."

"Sometimes we have to make decisions using our mind not our heart" ~ uncle

CHAPTER 7

#DREAMCHASER

Rion's One Word

D- Discipline outworks motivation

R- Rely on yourself to make it happen for yourself

E- Earn your way

A- Achieve every goal you set

M- Manage your time wisely

C- Create opportunities for yourself

H- Have purpose

A- Action speaks louder than words

S- Shake off any obstacles that come your way

E- Empty your crowded mind, focus on the vision

R- Remember why you started

GROW THROUGH WHAT YOU GO THROUGH

Rion Cruz

Entrepreneur, Performance Coach, Mentor, and Advocate for
Financial Empowerment

The mission and vision behind what I do is to help impact
communities and the next generation. This is solely driven by the
great opportunity and freedom I have been blessed with in this
lifetime to be able to pursue anything I envision for myself. I truly
believe that we all have a designated purpose to fulfill and a fire to
ignite to do great things beyond measure for others, ourselves, and
the world. With that being said, I am very passionate and dedicated
to help make a positive shift in underserved communities around the
world and in the United States through my works of
entrepreneurship, advocacy, and mentorship.

My overall mission is to help bridge the financial/wealth gap in
today's generation, especially within the youth, through my long-
term goal to help innovate learning opportunities by creating
educational platforms and programs that will serve a wide range of
demographics. As a coach and advocate for financial education, I
have an innate grasp to empower others through what I know.
Whether that'd be through financial literacy, entrepreneurship, or
general health. It is definitely a major passion of mine to help
facilitate personal growth amongst many individuals who seek
elevation and learning opportunities. Therefore, my aim is to be a
resource that changes lives for the better that will serve a greater
impact on a generation as a whole.

As for the coaching side of who I am, I have dedicated the past five
years in this field learning about general health, strength training, and
overall peak performance. This all truly stemmed from the process
of preparation for the sport that I played and loved, which was
football. Ever since my freshman year of high school, I took a
serious interest in sports medicine and various health sciences. I
always knew training and nutrition went hand in hand in the off-

season, but I truly did not know the depths behind its purpose and importance. So, I began doing self-research on learning about the human body and how performance training can drastically improve athletic performance and overall quality of life for oneself. This made me curious and eager to explore, and so I was very experimental, applying everything and anything I learned to carve my path for growth.

Of course, various obstacles and mistakes were made along the way, but that's where all the learning and growing occurs, and that's why becoming a coach was an easy decision for me to make. I knew deep down that I could do something with this passion and help pave a clearer path for others who desire to reach their goals with their health. Ultimately, once I knew I was ready to take on that responsibility, the discipline and willingness to learn elevated to the next level.

I am now a certified coach from the National Academy of Sports Medicine (NASM), and I am currently running my coaching business in Southern California. I have helped over 25 individuals from different backgrounds, each with all the same common goals of getting stronger, instilling a more active lifestyle, and improving overall quality of life. I specialize in strength training, weight loss, nutrition planning, and sports performance. Therefore, my next main goal is to expand and innovate my coaching business to help many more individuals on a larger scale around the world.

There are a lot of negative stigmas that surround social media as a whole. However, on a positive reflection, in this generation, social media has been taken to new heights and has been used to innovate the world of technology to where everything and anything can be accessible to everyone. In relation to this, social media has made a large impact in any field, especially entrepreneurship. Social media has provided many individuals with access to a diverse range of resources in an instant, and it has provided ways for people to learn anything at the tip of their fingers. In my opinion, it has helped me branch out my knowledge by exposing me to many different people who are devoted to their craft in their respective industries. From financial literacy, e-commerce, real estate, and even personal training/coaching, social media has been a prime mover in my process to gain more insight into these things which has facilitated growth in my knowledge.

We all face pivotal moments in life, and I remember this phase of life like it was yesterday. During this time, many situations and instances happened that changed the course of my personal life and our family's situation. However, this pivotal time truly helped me discover and realize many different things about the mindset shift and perspective change that I needed to make for myself. This changed me for the better, and I now see clearer with an open mind, forever motivated to carry this on throughout the rest of my life with a perspective that I hope everyone has or gravitates to instill. With that being said, the story begins.

It was still early in 2020, around the beginning of March when my family and I got the notification that my mom's father, my grandfather, had been rushed to the emergency after a severe fall that would alter and change the course of the rest of his life. I remember finishing up a workout at the gym with my younger brother when I received a text message from my mom that there was a family emergency and that we were getting picked up immediately. I was in complete shock; it was so unexpected. Many different thoughts flooded my mind, mostly concerns and worries.

As soon as we got in the car my mom told us that we are making an emergency road trip back to our hometown of Vancouver, Canada, where my grandfather and most of our family members resided. As soon as we got back to the house, we packed up and gathered everything we knew we needed to embark on this long trip ahead in hopes of finding sanity and relief that everything was going to be okay. I remember us leaving our house early in the morning the next day, sometime around 4 am. It was still pitch-black outside.

As we were pulling out of the driveway, I remember looking back. I was curious, but rather more worried about how long we were going to be gone and what the circumstance of my grandfather was. However, little did we know, we were making the trip at a very uncertain time. The news finally broke out about the Coronavirus spreading rapidly through the United States as we were driving. We then found out about the announcement that school was getting canceled for the next two weeks until further notice. This is where panic began to arise around the world, not knowing that it would change everyone's lives forever.

All this happened in such an instant, but we held tight and just kept moving forward to our main goal, which was to get to our grandfather. Fast forward, we arrive and make it to Canada safely, and we are able to see my grandfather at the local hospital in Vancouver. As soon as we walked into the room where he was bedridden, emotion and concern immediately filled the atmosphere. It was a tough pill to swallow, seeing our beloved grandfather who was just fine two months back in critical condition. I remember him not being able to speak or move. He was only able to communicate by shaking his head in a yes and no manner, but we made the most out of it, not knowing that it would be the last time that we would ever get to be with him.

Looking back, I remember vividly leaving the hospital with a complete change in emotion and feeling. I was downhearted by this whole situation, but I realized something that changed me for the rest of my life. Going through this specific time and phase in life with my family taught me a lot. It taught me that taking things for granted will catch up to you because life is so short it can take anything in an instant. Learn to appreciate it more often and don't overlook its worth. It truly opened up my eyes to see a different perspective through what we have in life. I've always been the type of person who's been eager to get to the next step, in other words, the next chapter. I always wanted to see what was on the other side of that next page in my book and what step was going to be in line. Oftentimes, especially during the transition from Vancouver to Los Angeles, I was impatient, but in a good way. However, it got to the point where I was sometimes bitter because I felt like the process of transitioning to that next chapter was happening slowly and that pursuing my goals was so far away. I felt like I wasn't even close to the next step of starting my journey. I wanted everything to happen so fast on my terms in a blink of an eye so that I could feel fulfilled and move forward. However, this experience of witnessing this unfortunate situation with my grandfather made me realize that the appreciation of life and loving the people around us need more attention.

We often get so caught up with living the life that we want, the goals we aim to achieve, and the abundance we desire. However, while all of those things are good, we tend to forget about the present moment and that which is irreplaceable. We lose sight of what's right in front of us. In other words, the life that's in front of us. Going through this phase in life made me realize that I was losing sight of certain things right in front of me. I wasn't appreciating the present and the people who were around me enough. I was taking everything for granted because I was so focused on the next big step. I was losing sight of enjoying the process and appreciating every single day. So, it came down to seeing my beloved grandfather in critical condition in the hospital; it was a wake-up call to see that family is truly everything and that the ones who love and care for you aren't going to be here forever.

It's essential to believe in the importance that family comes first over everything. There's always a fine balance between working on your journey and yourself but also never letting that get in the way of remembering your roots, where you came from, and the people who have supported you since the beginning. Therefore, take it for what it's worth, take every moment in, and appreciate life for everything that it comes to be because it goes quickly. Work hard, but learn to slow down, enjoy life, and love everyone closest to you with full passion.

My vision for the future always relates to fulfilling my purpose through what I do. The ultimate goal is to be a key resource and to have the platform to give back to many communities through educational resources and opportunities for career, entrepreneurial, and personal growth. Aside from that, my personal vision for the future is to keep growing and improving in all aspects of life. Whether that be mentally, spiritually, or physically, every day is an opportunity for me to put in the work to become the best version of myself. Therefore, the ultimate vision is to keep climbing to create opportunities for myself and reach my greatest potential.

Quotes I live by:

A quote that I live by is from one of the biggest motivational speakers in the world and an inspiration to many. I remember watching Inky Johnson for the very first time. It was around the beginning of 9th grade when I was embarking on my new journey of being a student-athlete in California. I had many different feelings and thoughts about my journey and the path that this whole process was taking me on. I didn't know what to expect, but I was just obsessed with the one goal in mind, which was to succeed in what I was pursuing. However, I always knew that my journey was going to be different from others. I always knew that God had a plan for me in what vision I had set out for myself and that it was going to be a difficult thing to trust. However, I always had the mindset of "keep moving forward" no matter what happens. This quote defines what trusting the process means and that everything will fall into place.

"Eventually you'll end up where you need to be, surrounded with who you're meant to be with and Impact who you're meant to Inspire." - Inky Johnson

My one word is Dreamchaser.

The meaning of this word is very apparent, and it's very plain and simple when it comes to the basic definition. It's a word used to describe a person with the courage to follow their heart and the belief to succeed in the path that they take. It can mean many different things, and it can hold a diverse combination of what it takes to succeed in that journey. For me, being a dreamchaser is being relentless and persevering through everything that's against you. A dreamchaser does everything they can in their hands to accomplish whatever vision they set out for themselves. Being a dreamchaser is having a winner's mindset, a mindset that you know you have the ability and opportunity to reach greatness, so why sleep when you can chase and work to obtain it.

CHAPTER 8

#GRATEFUL

Sanju's One Word

G- Grow more but be grateful for everything

R- Respect everyone irrespective of one's age, gender, wealth, or preferences

A- Attitude is everything

T- Take initiative without hesitation, no matter what

E- Execution and over planning

F- Faith in the universe and God's plan

U- Understand that you're capable enough for anything you wish to achieve

L- Love your parents

Young Changemakers

EFFORT DOESN'T GET RECOGNIZED, ONLY SUCCESS DOES

"Sometimes God destroys your plans because he has better plans for you, so just trust him." - Sanju Kahuja

Parents spend thousands of dollars on academic fees in the hope that one day their children will be doing a dream job, be happy, self-dependent, living their dream life, driving their dream car, and satisfied with life. However, the reality is children end up getting jobs that are not of their interests, exhausting, and not that fulfilling. This is the *Digital Era* and things are easier than they used to be, and can be done with fewer resources, from the comfort of home, with options available according to one's interests and with exposure, without any academic or age boundaries.

I help aspiring young people generate income streams, with money making skills that interest them and help them achieve their dream lifestyle, by working on social media platforms they like most. It's my way of contributing back to the world, because when someone earns a living by doing what they love, it makes them happy and grateful. This way not only will the economy develop but also there'd be a vibration of love, happiness, and gratitude.

I feel privileged being able to understand the real potential of social media. Social media has the power to let one become independent and achieve their dream lifestyle. Being a school going student, no one allowed me to work or get exposure, and my parents felt I was too young, and the world is too big.

Then somehow, I learned how to make money using social media. On the day I hit the mark of 100K INR, I felt grateful and saw there were many students puzzled about how to make money using social media. I saw a need and therefore fulfilled it by mentoring them. To this day, I have mentored 2500+ students in one and a half years. I have interviewed 25+ authors from all over the world just because I knew it would bring me greater potential.

While in 10th grade, I came to learn about "Gratitude" for the first time, and I started practicing it on a daily basis. That year I topped the school with 95%, which was unexpected, since before that I used to fail. It's rightly said that if you're grateful for whatever you have, the universe is going to multiply it many times over. In today's era, most of us have the habit of complaining and complaining is considered the biggest sin of humans, as it is quoted in most holy books, and the day I got to know about such concepts, it changed my life.

One might think I'm too young to experience depression, but I have gone through that phase three times already in my life. However, even in the worst phase of my life, I was thankful to God for getting me into depression because I had learned many lessons the hard way and that everything happens for a reason. Unfortunately, though, we humans are not able to understand it. After some time, I realized that depression taught me detachment, solitude and not expecting anything, and that is the beauty of it. Buddha says, "Expectations are the root cause of sorrow," and I felt it.

The second pivotal time was when I entered into the marketing business, and no one was by my side. I faced a lot of criticism. Everyone around me was saying things like, "You're greedy for money at such a young age. - Focus on your studies. - You're distracted," etc. At that time, I was 17 and relatives started criticizing me; friends distanced themselves from me, and I was all alone. I just wouldn't listen, and I'm glad I didn't. By the time I generated my first one-hundred dollars, wouldn't you know, everyone suddenly started connecting, and appreciated what I was doing. They even began asking me to teach their children how to do it too!

I learned this journey of becoming something is hard, and everyone must do it all alone, but the day you are successful, everyone will be by your side. Loving yourself, believing in your potential, hard work and God's plan for you, are going to make you successful. Don't ever let yourself down just because someone said something to you. Remember those people who criticize you or complain are doing it because they haven't made it big. Also, love your parents; they're your only true supporters. Be grateful for everything, whether good or bad. Trust me; it's going to change your life drastically for the better!

I have two visions for my future. Firstly, helping 100k people generate revenue streams using social media. Second, gratitude and spirituality have a great influence in my life, so I want to spread the word about its importance, as I believe foundational principles of all religions are similar to that of humanity, and we as humans are not aware of this.

Quotes I live by...

"Everything happens for a good cause, be it good or bad" - Sanju Kahuja

"Sometimes God destroys your plans because he has better plans for you, so just trust him." - Sanju Kahuja

"Expectations are the root cause of all sorrows."- Buddha

CHAPTER 9

#CHANGE

Manasi's One Word

C- Challenge your limits

H- Hold hope in your heart when it seems to get
gloomy all over

A- Always be ready to accept failure

N- Nothing can truly hold you back except the walls
of your mind

G- Go after your dreams because you grow the most
in the process

E- Enjoy the journey, you will never get a chance to
do it again in the same manner

DOING THE HARD THINGS REPEATEDLY BUILDS CONFIDENCE EVENTUALLY

It isn't enough just talking about problems. We need actions, and we need changemakers. - Manasi Patil

Young Changemaker, Public Speaker, GenZ Youth Advocate

I believe in the power of youth, and how every teenager has an undefined potential to impact a change in their community. GenZ is a force that can change the way we perceive problems across the globe and partake in fresh perspectives on finding solutions. My mission is to reinforce GenZ potential, and I am keen to have as many GenZ'ers as possible find their light circling around their passion, talents, and skills, and help the world shine a little brighter. As a writer and public speaker, I spread awareness through my writings in magazines, publications, and my two published books. With my TED talk, and views shared at events, social gatherings, and workshops in schools and colleges, I hope to reach millions of teenagers, as I feel the encouragement to begin, and continue, is crucial for any impact to transpire.

Social media is surfacing more and more like a bridge from one thing to another. In my opinion, how you use social media has the power to either make or break your life. Just like a coin with two sides, social media has brought forward umpteen instances where it has failed us, as well as led us to impactful change. For my part, social media has definitely aided me a lot, mostly in being able to reach teenagers, and young changemakers, across the globe with my message and collaborations. Observing so many teenagers using social media, I realized that social media definitely could change your life, and it is only up to you as to how you interact with it.

In my primary school, I was a very involved kid, participating in all the activities my school held: elocutions, dance, singing, mono-acting, you name it. However, there were very few times I actually won any of them. I used to practice a lot, but the moment I went on stage, my confidence shattered, and the only thought running around my mind was that of getting off the stage. All the preparation I had done became my secondary thought, and my efficiency rate was only about 45-50 percent. My mother, however, never let this get to me, and every time when I returned from any contest, without a trophy, she always made me sit beside her and said, what has been etched on my soul forever. I was taught then, how life is about living for the best parts, because the worst parts are inevitable, and that there's more beauty and value in the *'in-betweens'* than I ever gave credit to. It's about doing things repeatedly that builds your confidence eventually, and by losing a hundred times, you gain experiences and perspectives on the win you'd never get anywhere else. Perhaps this was the lesson through all her words over the years that shaped me and my confidence.

It isn't enough just talking about problems. We need actions, and we need changemakers. My vision for GenZ and the future is for every teenager to recognize the light in themselves, grab hold of it, and let it lead their way forth to go a step ahead and contribute to adding this light in the community, to a world where every teenager feels comfortable using their talent and skills to impact a change.

Quotes I live by:

Don't watch the clock; do what it does. Keep going. ~ *Sam Levenson*

Be the change that you wish to see in the world. ~ *Mahatma Gandhi*

CHAPTER 10

I WISH I KNEW THEN…

By Glenn Marsden

Thinking about what I wish I knew then and pondering thoughts as to what I should write about, ended up being the very thing I thought I shouldn't write about.

Confusing you yet?

Well, for starters, I am in my logic, I am trying to conjure up in my mind, what I think you all need to hear reading my words rather than simply allowing the words to merely flow through my spirit and onto the page before me.

This right here is the very thing I wish that I knew back then – finding faith.

A faith in me, myself, a faith in God, that I never knew existed back then. To experience total surrender to allowing myself to just be. To not try to control aspects of my life, well if I am honest, nearly all my life, throughout my younger years.

We all do it, from what we think we need our appearance should be like to fit in, how we present ourselves, how we sound, who we need to associate with, who we think we need to be like, what we should like, who we should like, what job we think we should do, caring about what others will think of us.

The list goes on and we all know it does, but it can and will become a minefield of danger if we allow it to take over our lives. I did for some time there when I was younger.

For some reason unbeknownst to me I sought validation about my appearance. I picked myself apart, I put unrealistic pressure on myself to try to be perfect. I presented myself daily to those around me with a smile, yet inside even as a guy who grew up hearing through the media airwaves, we had to mask our emotions, we had to be strong, I was struggling.

Struggling with conflict in my mind.

I didn't know which way to turn and the more I thought I could control these ever-present thoughts about perfectionism with my body, the more I was realizing I was losing the battle.

You see, it took me to hit rock bottom to find my escape from my own mind!

How crazy does that sound, right!

I was forced in to letting go of that control, I was forced into a position of breaking down and sobbing like a child feeling like nothing on the floor....

Until,

I was picked up by those around me that loved me. That simply held me and told me everything would be ok.

Perhaps, that was a sign sent straight from God that day that I was unaware of because I was simply never brought up with an environment of faith. However, that day, that embrace of love, that warmth showed me that I mattered and that amount of love shown to me that very day, opened my eyes to just how powerful the human touch, the human connection is when we allow it to come to us.

That right there I know now, is God, that's faith, that's the faith he has in us and more importantly the faith he puts in others to see us when we don't see ourselves.

That story is mine, that story I sit on, has gone on to inspire so many people out there that were waiting to hear it and they are waiting on yours too.

Life is a journey of lessons and once we learn to let go of trying to control everything and surrender more to open our eyes to what is important, I mean truly important, making memories, being grateful for what we do have, building friendships, forming relationships, being present in those moments, hey even in those moments of silence, learn to embrace all of it.

Through a media lens, through our TV screens to the radio's airwaves, our minds can be filled with those moments of trying to be something we are not, or unhappy with ourselves, merely because of what we see or hear that are often manipulated images we are shown, or marketing led to make us believe something to buy.

I just wish I knew what I know now of having that FAITH.

Faith to discern what I was being shown and hearing was real or not, faith to trust in myself, my own abilities, faith in something more to life out there to have belief in, faith in who I was, my imperfections and all.

So, my one word is Imperfect.

You see, as I sign off here, I want every person reading my words to know that you were made perfect just the way you were. We are all Imperfectly Perfect. There were no mistakes when you were created, yet through life, our eyes, our ears, our minds take in so much noise that at times we lose ourselves, the real us. The authentic us, the us that God made us to be.

As you go through your journey, I hope my words are brought to the forefront of your mind, should you ever lose your way and know that no matter what you encounter on your path, you are enough, you love those imperfections in yourself, and you have faith.

Faith in yourself and a faith in something higher than us all that will be right by your side when you call.

That for me is something I tell you; I wish I would've known back then and had somebody tell me.

CHAPTER 11

Young Changemakers

#EMPATHY

Anagha's One Word

E- Embrace your unique identity

M- Meet and connect with new people

P- Persevere even when the going gets hard

A- Aim for the moon and beyond

T- Trust your journey

H- Hope is the key to thriving in these difficult times

Y- Yock at yourself when you fall, gently pick yourself up, and keep going

YOURS UNSTOPPABLY

Anagha Rajesh

Undergraduate Researcher, Storyteller, and Community Builder

I spend a lot of time thinking about my mission and how I can contribute to the world. I have embraced the fact that there is no simple answer. As I evolve, the projects I take up also evolve, and my mission keeps expanding. At the moment, I lead *Yours Mindfully*, a team of 40+ young people on a mission to make mental health resources accessible to 1 million young people by 2030. I work with Force of Nature as a climate consultant to help companies across the globe switch to sustainable business models, and I am a Venture Capital Associate with gradCapital helping student founders raise funds for bold startup ideas.

Academically, I am pursuing an undergraduate degree in chemistry and am working on research projects in biochemistry, neuroscience, and entrepreneurship. In addition, I spend a lot of time reading, traveling, and having fun with the literary and debating club at my university. When I look at all of the initiatives I am involved in, an underlying theme emerges - unstoppable. I want to be unstoppable. I want to build a world where every individual is unstoppable in their own right.

I am the first person in my family to get accepted into a top-tier university in India. I am the first woman in my family and community to build and lead a non-profit. As cool as it sounds, it is insanely hard to be the first. You have no pre-existing networks or mentors to help you locate the right resources.

Social media has been my portal to connect with other youngsters pursuing similar goals, reach out to potential mentors, and access resources from across the globe. I found many of my team members at *Yours Mindfully* through Instagram and LinkedIn. We found a lot of collaborators, advisors, and sponsors through social media channels. In addition, we put out resource packs on burnouts and media exposure during crises through social media to make it accessible and affordable to young people. This could not have happened without it.

At the same time, I have fallen down the social media rabbit holes many times. I mindlessly scroll through content and compare myself with the best versions of others. In the last few months, I have taken a lot of social media breaks because of burnout. Recently, a young girl reached out to me after I wrote about one of my achievements. She said that I have been lucky to get here and that she can never even dream of doing half the things I do. That really broke my heart. I realized that by sharing snapshots of just my happiest moments, I am contributing to a more significant problem. So, I have started writing more honestly and openly about my stories on social media. I try to bring my authentic self into my content, including the failures and the moments of self-doubt. I hope that by doing this it helps other young people connect better with my story and motivates them to bring their authentic selves to social media platforms.

Life is made of many moments that have a significant impact on becoming who you are. There are three important moments that have shaped who I am.

The 4-Year-Old Storyteller

In kindergarten, I was a rebellious child. I refused to walk in a line or sit quietly in a class. I troubled the other kids by snatching their tiffin boxes to figure out what snacks they had, and my teacher was annoyed. So, she did what most teachers would do and called up my parents to complain about me. Amma knew she had to do something about it, and she came up with a master plan by signing me up for a storytelling contest. She channeled all my energy into understanding the story of the greedy dog who lost his bone to his reflection in the river. She got me to narrate the story in my style. This was the first time I was going to speak for such a long duration in English. I had been speaking only my mother tongue, Malayalam, until then. This was my first tryst with public speaking. I loved how people in the audience were listening to me. It felt good, despite the nervousness. I think that's when I discovered that I have a voice and that I can use it to tell stories that matter. Of course, this realization came much later when I connected the dots, but for little Anagha, it was just about having fun with the doggy costume!

My Uncle and Schizophrenia

This part of my lived experience drives a large chunk of the work I do. I grew up in a family where mental health conversations were swept under the rug. My uncle suffered silently from schizophrenia for over 10 years until he could access psychiatric support. There was a stigma associated with my uncle's condition. He faced isolation, and this initially made me curious about the human brain and why conditions of the brain are not treated the same as conditions of the rest of the body. When I spoke about this to a few girls I met as a part of the 1000 Girls 1000 Futures mentorship program of the New York Academy of Science, my life flipped by 180 degrees. We began working on e-magazines to create awareness about mental health, and over the last three years, this e-magazine project has grown into a youth-led organization with 40+ members and some incredible mentors. We have managed to impact 10,000+ youngsters globally and are on a mission to impact 1 million by 2030. Drawing from experience to create impact initiatives is one of our world's most powerful driving forces. I am so glad I discovered it early on in life.

Having to Pick a College Major

As a middle and high school student, I had diverse interests. I loved everything from poetry to science experiments. I was flabbergasted when I had to choose universities and figure out what subject I wanted to major in. I did not want to leave behind any of my interests, and I felt like a loser because everyone around me seemed to know what majors they wanted to do. I experienced an intense fear that if I left a particular subject behind right now, I could never return to it. That's when I came across Emilie Wapnick's TED Talk '*Why Don't Some of Us Have One True Calling?*' It is about people with multipotentiality personalities and how this kind of personality goes underrated in a world that values specialization. I began following the Puttyverse, a community of multipotentialities from across the globe. Listening to their stories made me feel less lonely on my journey. (P.S. this is probably the only thing I have in common with

Aristotle, Da Vinci, and Maya Angelou.) I ended up picking a university that allows me to explore a wide range of domains regardless of my major, and I love it! This experience taught me how important a community is to realize one's true identity and potential.

So, what does the road ahead look like for me? My vision is to work at the intersection of STEM, entrepreneurship, and public policy to make the world more inclusive. This includes bringing more women into domains they have traditionally been excluded from, making mental health accessible and tailoring educational resources that enable students with disabilities to pursue education.

Quotes I live by...

"What's truer than the truth? It's the story." - Jewish Proverb.

I believe that the stories we tell shape our individual and societal perspectives. For instance, we can forgive ourselves better when our self-talk is rooted in kindness. We can address many of the world's biggest challenges by reframing the narratives around power and agency. When a select group controls the narratives around what is possible, it becomes tough for those who look and speak differently to bring their solutions to the table. This quote beautifully captures what it takes to drive individual and systemic change, and that's why I love it so much!

CHAPTER 12

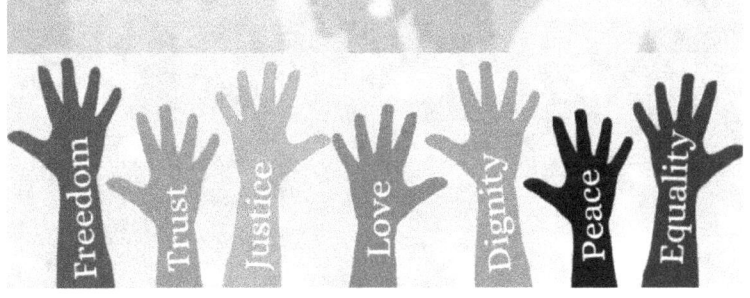

HUMANITY

"The purpose of human life is to serve, to have compassion and the will to help others."

Freedom Trust Justice Love Dignity Peace Equality

#HUMANITY
Siddhita's One Word

H- Have faith in yourself

U- United we stand, divided we fall

M- Make the world a better place to live

A- Action speaks louder than words

N- No discrimination

I- Interact with more people

T- Take the initiative

Y- Your attitude matters a lot

THE JOURNEY TO CHANGE

"Never stop learning because life never stops teaching." - *Siddhita Mohanty*

Graphic Designer, Digital Entrepreneur, Innovator,
Public Speaker, and Android App Developer

I want to serve people to improve their mental health as a world class medical scientist. My objective is to use the creative talents of young minds to develop digital products using graphic design through my company Bloom Riddhi Siddhi (BRS) and implement the concept of 'earn while you learn' to supplement financial assistance to aspiring students having interest in graphic design. I aspire to promote billions of talented children from around the globe in formative school years in this exciting area of graphic design to improve the economic status of their country by using their creative talents. I also have an idea to build 10,000+ orphanages and old age homes so that old parents can be in the company of children and children can get the affection of parents.

Social media plays a very vital role in all of our lives and so it did in mine. I remember two years back, during the pandemic when there was a terror about the noble Coronavirus everywhere and people were going through a lot of mental pressure like stress and depression, due to the increase of Covid-19 cases in the thousands. Every single day was filled with fear as people were losing their loved ones, more people were getting infected, and many people even lost their jobs. Social media was the tool which was creating a lot of anxiety among people. I have seen my friends and family members sharing the number of Covid cases of that day, how to keep themselves away from Coronavirus, etc., through different social media like WhatsApp and Facebook.

However, if we turn this around, many people use social media to showcase their talents, connect with new people, etc. So, social media (especially LinkedIn) was really beneficial for me as I was able to connect with people from all over the world by just sitting in one place. I started working with them, learned different things and gained a lot of inspiration from a new network of incredible people, and I attended online classes on different topics without moving anywhere. I think the most remarkable achievement was when I opened my own digital startup named Bloom Riddhi Siddhi (BRS) by gaining inspiration from my fellow LinkedIn connections.

My journey started at an early age of 2, when my parents gave me a laptop on my 2nd birthday. Since my childhood, I used to watch many English cartoons, movies, and rhymes. I used to do a lot of digital paintings using MS Paint and Tux Paint. I was studying at a school in Odisha named "St. Luke's School, Burla." Though I was doing well in academics, I was having no extra knowledge. I never thought of anything other than studies and always thought of myself. I remember I wasn't even able to speak a sentence in English properly. We used to study almost ten subjects, Math, Science, Social Science, English, Hindi (Regional Language of India), Odia (Our local language- spoken in Odisha), Art education, Computer Science, Gk and Value education. Other than that, we had Yoga and PE (Physical Education) which included Kabaddi, Football and Cricket (for boys) and Kho-kho and Dodgeball (for girls). Yes, this is how it was classified and that's the reason why most of the girls of our school faced discrimination, but no one ever spoke up against it.

I'm glad that I wasn't one of them because I raised my voice for my rights every single time, even if I faced a lot of problems. Due to this, many of my teachers liked me a lot because I was walking on the path of moral values. Even after all of this none of us were having life skills and courage to face real life situations. To be honest, this was not the kind of school life that I wanted for my childhood. After all, I had fun in my school as I was one of the oldest students at that school as I started studying there from pre-school and ended up in grade 7, but wait, here's the game changer… Covid-19.

The Coronavirus came, and we were all locked in our homes. As I mentioned earlier, there were two types of people during Covid-19, those who kept on worrying about the pandemic and those who tried to utilize this period to enhance their skills and show their talents. I am very grateful that I was the second type of person because Covid-19 was one of the turning points in my life. Let's find out how.

So, with the increase in Covid cases, the lockdown started. During the lockdown in the year 2020, I remember my online classes were going on during the morning hours from 8 am to 12 pm (Monday-Friday). Except for these four hours, I was sitting idle playing some games or doing some sketching. Then, one day when my mom was surfing through the internet, she found a coding course offered by Whitehat Jr. So, my parents registered for that course, and my coding classes began. I found coding quite interesting and after some time couldn't believe my eyes! The time I was wasting here was converted to attending more online classes because by that time I used to sit for 10-12 hours to do coding. OMG!!! What a surprise! I never ever imagined that I would be introduced to the world of coding. I was even among the top 50 rankers in Whitehat Jr.

After a few months, my dad enrolled me in a course on Higher Order Thinking Skills (HOTS). There I got an amazing mentor who motivated and supported me a lot. Also, I did a lot of courses on spoken English from the British Council. By the end of the year, I achieved a global rank of 26th and 40th in the International Ethics and Values Olympiad (IEVO) and International Life Skills Olympiad (ILSO) organized by Skillzen Foundation, Singapore. There were almost 20,000+ participants from about 100+ countries. I can say that this was my first milestone because I appeared for ILSO the first time in 2019 and was ranked 556.

New year, new beginnings, new experiences, and new things to learn. The year 2021 got started, and I learned a lot more. I still can't believe my eyes that I learned almost 10+ skills during the year 2021 like coding (block coding and android app development), public speaking, 21st century skills, memory techniques, robotics, entrepreneurship, python coding, gaming, web design, NLP, French, book writing, Badminton and the list goes on, but wait, this was not the end. In April 2021, my father introduced me to LinkedIn, and I really liked it. I started doing digital 3D designs, and after a few weeks, I had 128 connections over LinkedIn, 50+ 3D designs, 3 jobs in different organizations and a lot of support from my LinkedIn family. The organization which helped me the most was The Clippers Child Council of India (TCCCI). I was actually a board member there, and I got a lot of inspiration and support from my colleagues. In the same month, I got admitted to Orchids, the

International School (Nagarbhavi Branch). As the admission process was online, I wasn't supposed to travel to Bangalore. When my online classes were going on in the month of May, we had an online event at school on the auspicious occasion of Mother's Day. All the students were asked to make something for their mother and present it on Mother's Day. I remember it was May 9, 2021. I created an animation which included all my memories with my mom since my birth, and everyone was just flabbergasted by seeing my creativity. That was my first step in the world of Graphic Design.

Since my childhood, I used to create a lot of PPTs and pictures. Also, throughout my childhood, I was fascinated by seeing the images of big, luxurious houses and their interior designs, but this one was my first milestone in the wonderful area of Graphic design. By the month of August, I did 2 events and 1 interview. In September, I got selected for the Global Youth Education Summit (YES). It was conducted internationally and there were almost 100+ speakers from across 35+ countries. It was organized by Aunua Academy, Ireland. That was the first event in which I was represented globally. My topic was "Joy of Mental Well-Being." I remember, my father and I sat till 3 am to write and record the speech. I think that was one of the most memorable moments of my life. With the upcoming of October, came a lot of surprises, starting with October 11th, it was my 13th birthday, and guess what I opened? My own digital startup at the age of 13. WOW!!! What a kickstart to my teenage years. The event was organized by SkillShark EduTech, and it went really well. Also, I did my first internship at *The Talk Bar* in the month of October. By December, I was a part of the Asia CEO Community, and yes that's it for 2021, a very eventful year!

With the start of 2022, came great news. Starting in January, I got the opportunity to work in a superb web series named "Trouvaille". It was the world's first-ever historical web series created by children and was created by *The Clippers*. March was a month of success. First, I got world rank 6 in International Life Skills Olympiad (ILSO), rank 6 in International Values & Ethics Olympiad (IEVO), rank 12 in International Economic Skills Olympiad (IESO) and rank 14 in International Leadership Skills Olympiad (ILO). Secondly, I was awarded with the prestigious Women Power India Awards 2022 in the category of *'Girl Child Prodigy of the Year'* by Raj Square Charity Foundation and MIT Square, London.

By that time, I shifted to Bangalore. I was celebrated in my school, and it was my first media coverage. The pic of that event was in almost 10 newspapers. Lastly, I reached 1k followers over LinkedIn and BRS reached 100+ followers. After a few weeks, I was among one of the Global Youth Ambassadors at Aunua Academy, Ireland and the story goes on. So, from my story I just wanted to share the message that the journey to change will never be easy but keep up the good work and work hard for it and you will surely achieve it one day.

My vision for the future is to emerge as a Global Leader to serve for the well-being of the society as I will be contributing my whole life for the betterment of mankind and to make this world a better place to live in. I aspire to graduate from the University of Oxford with a major in medicine in the emerging field of neuroscience and minor in architecture. Also, I am working to make my startup become one of the best in the world so that I can provide employment to more and more people to reduce unemployment. I also see myself as a leader who can make women feel that they are all safe in this world, help the poverty rate to be at its lowest and the literacy rate be at its highest so that no one ever struggles to educate their children, keep their family happy, and sleep with an empty belly. I see myself as a person who can make people realize that every single person in this world is equal no matter what they are, who they are or what their salary is. They should never have the perspective that people can be categorized based on their caste, color, gender, religion, creed, status, nationality, etc. Instead, they should have a viewpoint that all of us fall under just one category that is humanity because we all have the same life, and before this we are first and foremost a human being.

Quotes I live by…

"Education is the most powerful weapon you can use to change the world."
- Nelson Mandela

"There are three powers in this world, the first one is the power of sword, second is the power of pen and the third one is the power of women which is stronger than all." - Malala Yousafzai

CHAPTER 13

Growth
Mindset

IM ·· POSSIBLE

"Success is how willing you
are to not get the result you
are looking for."

Sarah Syed

#MINDSET

Sarah's One Word

M – Mistakes are made to learn from

I – I can improve through hard work

N – Never Give Up

D – Determination is necessary

S – Success comes from self-reflection

E – Effort will help me see improved results

T – Try your best no matter what

WHAT WILL YOUR STORY AND YOUR IMPACT LOOK LIKE?

Sarah Syed

Climate Activist, Innovator, and Poet

As a young climate activist, innovator, and poet, I want to inspire other youth to discover their passions, follow their curiosity and embark on the journey of becoming a leader; a changemaker. My goal is to encourage other young girls to pursue a career in STEM and combat the gender stereotypes associated with technology careers. Often youth are looked at as the future, yet time and time again we see young people taking a stand and fighting for what they believe in. I want to help youth realize the tools to create social change are in front of them, they just need to follow their intuition and find what makes them excited.

Over the past four years, I have been working on innovation within the sustainability space using emerging technology. I enjoy learning more about the technology that is currently being used to progress many systems from renewable energy to calculating ESG (Environment, Social and Governance) metrics. However, the three emerging technologies I am currently innovating in, and I enjoy learning more about, are material science, nanotechnology, and AI (artificial intelligence). I think one of the main reasons I was so enthralled by these spaces in science was because these three pieces of tech are a part of our everyday lives from the phones we use to the clothes we wear and items we use. For example, our healthcare industry is advancing every day because of nanotechnology.

A problem that struck me the most in the beginning was plastic pollution. Often, I would see plastic bags on trees and on the occasion a piece of plastic on a seagull or bird's foot. According to *Our World in Data*, 380 million tons of plastic is thrown away yearly and some sources claim that 100 million animals die each year from plastic waste alone. I realized plastic production had a greater detriment than just impacting ecosystems. As stated in *National Geographic*, a recent study by Vethaak and his colleagues found

101

plastics in the blood. I began to research ways of making biodegradable plastics from food scraps like banana peels, orange peels, potato peels and other peels high in starch. I am now building on this project as I am working to develop a biodegradable coffee-pod.

Something I prioritize when working on my innovations is sustainability, scalability, feasibility, and efficiency. Over the past two years, I have worked on a biodegradable bio-sorbent made from pomegranate and orange peels with an additional polysaccharide aerogel with a 98% efficiency in removing heavy metals, organic compounds, and oil from various bodies of water at varying temperatures. This project is close to my heart since I began to work on a bio-sorbent after I read an article about an oil spill happening near my home country.

I am pivoting from ocean pollution to renewable energies and researching how nanotechnology and artificial intelligence can design a rotating semi-transparent solar panel; like a sunflower, where the solar panel will move in the direction of the sun increasing the efficiency from the standard 22%. Among other innovations, I enjoy helping others realize that leaders are not born because anyone can be a leader. I have amassed over a thousand community hours supporting organizations that help youth gain insights on their preferred career choices and become changemakers. I volunteer with different organizations and help them with their mission of sustainability, social justice, and DEI.

Whether it be through public speaking or organizing community and international events, the process it took to reach my goals has been a bumpy one with many obstacles I needed to overcome. I faced challenges in the projects I worked on but the biggest reminder I love sharing with others is that challenges are the building blocks of success. Taking the unconventional path is a great feat but rewarding in the long-term progress. I am dedicated to helping youth discover their potential and be a part of the solution to the climate crisis through innovation, community action, and advocacy.

I like to describe social media using the analogy for technology. Technology is a powerful tool at our disposal, but it has the ability to do more harm than good. Needless to say, technology is also seen as a force of good. For example, solar panels to produce renewable energy can help make the transition smoothly to a fossil-fuel free world. Similarly, social media can inspire others, but it can also negatively impact individuals or groups. At the end of the day, it is up to the person who is using social media to decide whether they use it as a medium for good or for bad. I have chosen to use social media for good and speak awareness on climate justice. Climate change is like a puzzle piece, we see the global image, but it is a symptom of many interrelated problems which are the sub-pieces of a puzzle. The lack of education contributes to climate change. Diversity, equity, and inclusion barriers are contributing to climate change. Social media has helped me talk more about these challenges and bring awareness to the reality of our planet.

As the founder of an international youth-led organization, *You Are the Change*, our mission is to help youth find their passion and tie it to solving a climate problem of their choice from ocean pollution to food waste using entrepreneurship, STEM, creative arts, etc. Social media has helped me connect with like-minded organizations and develop partnerships to organize an international environmental hackathon which had over 1000 participants and raised $200 to support an organization that is building a school in Africa (Green Schools Green Future). Social media has also given me multiple opportunities to share my story as a seasoned public speaker. Few of my opportunities have been from cold-messages sent to me through LinkedIn. One of the current projects *You Are the Change* is working on is a poetry contest and entrepreneurship, climate change conference, and I have the incredible opportunity to work alongside phenomenal youth to bring these projects to a reality. I have also been inspired by so many young leaders who are taking a stand to fight for a brighter, healthier, sustainable, and connected future.

A pivotal moment in my climate journey was when I was in grade four. I discovered in a global context what climate change is and its detrimental impacts contributing to the destruction of our only planet. Our teacher randomly chose global problems the class needed to do research on and create a presentation for the class. I discovered the heartbreaking, dystopian-like reality of our planet. From habitat loss to global temperatures rising to the exponentially increasing curve of greenhouse gas emissions and fossil fuel productions, we have steadily been on a path that is paved towards a cliff. Climate change is more than just the statistics but how decisions you and I take each day that contribute to these bigger pictures associated with the term climate change.

I still distinctly remember the worry and fear of not knowing what the future of our planet would be like if we even would have a planet to live on if humanity continued to live the same way as today. Actions do matter, even if they are of one individual. Imagine if the 8 billion people on this planet thought that their actions or their voice does not matter, we would have fallen into despair faster than the rate it took us to get to our current state of the planet. The world needs your actions times the 8 billion people on this planet.

I began my journey with small, token actions. For example, switching a plastic water bottle with a reusable one and encouraging my friends to make eco-friendly switches as well. I introduced a program at my elementary school known as the climate fact of the week to spread awareness on this critical issue. I volunteered in my community, organized school Earth Day events, facilitated clean-ups and supported youth-led initiatives. In grade 6, my class was asked to prepare a science fair project and present it to compete in the school science fair. My passion at the time being climate studies and environmental stewardship was paired with STEM. Participating in this science fair led me to realize that young people can become innovators, all it takes is a person's willingness to try. In class, we had done a chapter on battery pollution, and I wanted to see what could be done to remediate this problem and decided to experiment by creating a lemon battery. While this isn't relatively new, it gave me the self-confidence and motivation to pursue my dream as an innovator and start working on implementable projects that can be scaled in the future.

Ever since, I have worked on different projects in the field of STEM for the past four years starting since grade 9 and am working on a rotating solar panel currently. This journey has taught me that age is not a limitation but a superpower. As stated by many activists, we are not going to solve a problem as big as climate change with the same people who have caused it; we need the process of mitigating climate change to be an intergenerational one. Youth bring enthusiasm, creativity and different perspectives to the table which will lead to diverse solutions, and it is critical that youth be a part of the change they wish to see. However, I also learned the importance of moving beyond token actions and focusing on solutions. Continuing to make climate-conscious decisions is a great way to reduce your carbon footprint but by joining a group to amplify change or combine your passion to spread awareness, encourage others to take a stand or design solutions, we can move the dial further on palpitating climate change. Our passion can be the paintbrush to draw on our canvas tangible and actionable solutions and turn activism into a ripple effect inspiring hundreds around the world to fight for a better future, because change starts and ends with you.

Lastly, working on the project in grade 6 and the different projects throughout the past 4 years have taught me the importance of having a growth mindset and the power of consistency. Simply put, success is not your willingness to try but rather how willing you are to not get the result you are looking for. On the other hand, failure is standing idle in the face of a problem you can contribute a solution to. Anyone can be a climate activist but the question that you need to ask yourself is what do you want your story and your impact to look like?

My vision for the future is full of hope. Hope is the most important thing we need in order to progress. My vision is that youth will understand that age is not a limitation, it is a superpower. Additionally, this goes both ways to seniors as well. Actions speak louder than words. People will not remember you for your age but what actions you took instead. My vision is that we also work on better and more climate mitigation strategies which would be banning fossil fuels, helping those impacted the most by the climate crisis, transitioning to renewable energies and banning single-use plastics. We need to live in harmony with nature, not see nature as a reservoir for usage. The climate crisis gives us the opportunity to change the way we respond to global problems, therefore we need to come together as a global community and dedicate funding and time to save our only planet.

CHAPTER 14

Helpful

A NEW COMMAND
I GIVE YOU: LOVE
ONE ANOTHER. AS
I HAVE LOVED
YOU, SO YOU
MUST LOVE ONE
ANOTHER

#HELPFUL

Liza's One Word

H- Help others in need

E- Enjoy life

L- Laughing is the cure to sadness

P- Perseverance will get you far

F- Forgiving cures the heart

U- Use your mouth for kind words

L- Love everyone

NEW BEGINNINGS

Liza Magaña

Christian Singer, Aspiring Author

My mission is to help others reach their full potential through faith in Jesus, to help others understand there is hope, and that God has a purpose for everyone. I am contributing to the world by doing online groups for teens and tweens in Latin America and the United States, where I talk about my experiences and how God has helped me to overcome different situations.

I think social media is awesome, and like everything else, there are two sides to it. You can use it to encourage others, or you can use it to bring fear, doubt, and negativity. We just have to use it in a positive way. I use social media daily. It has impacted my life because it has helped me learn a lot. I get to hear other people's experiences, and I get to help other people through it. I'm working on building a Christian platform where I talk about my experiences.

I came to the United States 6 days before turning 13, and everything happened so fast with no time to say goodbye and process everything in my mind. I had to leave my home, country, school, pets, friends, and my family. Everything I knew and that was familiar to me. Everything that I grew up with was gone.

One of the hardest things for any human is to lose something that was always there, something that you loved. This can be even harder for a child or a teenager. Everything happened so fast when I moved to the United States, and I had to involve myself in different things and pray for strength, because I had to basically start over, and I felt that something was missing. I felt I didn't belong.

As I looked around me every day, I saw many people my age with their friends, going out, having fun, and it was like a reminder that I needed to start over again. Every new beginning is hard, but those hard times are needed, they build character and self-confidence. While I may have felt alone, I was able to turn to my faith. It was here that I learned I wasn't alone. I learned about someone who

111

wouldn't leave; I learned that someone loved me unconditionally, and that someone is Jesus.

The past year made me truly appreciate life. Life can change from one day to another, and to be truly happy in life, you have to have perspective. I now don't look back at what I lost. I look at what I gained. Being alone made me grow in faith, and I realized everything happens for a reason. I had to go on a long journey where I experienced a lot of stuff, many different emotions and experiences. Many times, I wished someone was there for me, and now that I look back, I realize that person was Jesus. That's what I want everyone to know. That is why I do these online groups and that is why I am writing this chapter, because that is what God sent us for, as it says in Hebrews 13:16, "And do not forget to do good and to share with others, for with such sacrifices God is pleased."

Being a teen or just a human in the world we live in today is hard. That's why if you help at least just one person you're already doing your part. You don't have to wait until you're an adult, there's no better time to start than this moment. Anything you can do is good enough. My purpose is to help others through my faith, and it's important to me because I know how rough life can get sometimes, so I want people to know there is someone who can help.

My vision for the future is to share with a bigger part of the youth that they aren't alone. I want to share with them that all the questions they have and all the confusion they may feel in this very moment have an answer. We all have a purpose, and it is in teaching them, that they will grow to understand what the perspective of life means.

A quote I live by:

"For we live by faith, not by sight." - 2 Corinthians 5:7

CHAPTER 15

#OVERCOME
Kristi's One Word

O - Only you have the strength within to meet the challenges you face.

V - Vision is what will keep you focused on what you want and where you want to go.

E - Every experience is a learning experience, good or bad. It's what you do with it that's important.

R - Resilience is key to staying the course after getting knocked down.

C - Courage comes from within to help you face adversities.

O - One opportunity at one moment is all it takes to turn your life around.

M - Make every day count as if it were your last.

E - Even when you feel like quitting, never give up.

I WISH I KNEW THEN…

It's not hard work, it's HEART work. Nothing is ever hard when it comes from the heart! – Kristi Maggio

Working on this project with these incredibly talented individuals made me realize so many things. I have learned more from them than they can even imagine, and in imparting to all youth what I wish I knew as a teenager and young adult, I leave the following:

1. Love yourself for who you are because the world would be a very boring place if we were all the same.

2. Don't look for attention in the wrong places by acting a certain way or being friends with the wrong people. Sometimes we do this because we think we are getting back at our parents, rebelling against them. However, in the end, the consequences can be more than expected. It can be hard to fit in but doing things that have irreversible consequences can be detrimental to the rest of your life. So, think before you act, and if it doesn't feel right, then don't do it. (I say this from personal experience, and I am lucky I survived.)

3. Ask for help from the right people, meaning those who have gone through or are doing what you want to do. You wouldn't ask a teacher about being a doctor, and you wouldn't ask business advice from someone who has never been in business. Seek the right people to mentor you along the way.

4. Nothing anyone can say or do can keep you from accomplishing your goals and dreams unless you allow them to!

5. Do not allow fear of failure or what other people think keep you from what you want to do. Although it can be difficult, ignore the naysayers. You can do whatever you set your mind to.

6. It doesn't matter where you are today or what your circumstances might be, focus on one thing you can do today to bring you to where you want to be.

7. When something doesn't go the way you thought it would, it doesn't mean that you weren't meant to do it. Failure is good if you learn from it; it is a part of life. We learn when we fail and must reflect on why. Then we go back and do it again, not making the same mistakes we did the first time. The only time you truly fail is when you quit.

8. Everyone has had struggles or roadblocks in their life. Your desire to accomplish your goals, your willingness to persevere, and your resilience when life is difficult will get you to where you want to be.

9. Don't compare yourself to those around you or other people on social media. The journey for everyone is unique. What we see is just a snapshot of what is really happening behind the scenes. Instant success rarely happens. Look at the stories of those you admire and research their journey. I guarantee it did not come overnight.

10. When you help and serve others, only then will you truly be fulfilled. It is when you know you can make a difference to the world around you that you will begin to feel love and happiness in your life.

Quotes I live by:

"And so I tell you, keep on asking, and you will receive what you ask for. Keep on seeking, and you will find. Keep on knocking, and the door will be opened to you. For everyone who asks, receives. Everyone who seeks, finds. And to everyone who knocks, the door will be opened."
— Jesus Christ, Luke 11:9-10

"Whether you think you can or think you can't, either way, you are right!"
— Henry Ford

"Why fit in when you were born to stand out!" — Dr. Seuss

It's not hard work, it's HEART work. Nothing is ever hard when it comes from the heart! — Kristi Maggio

AFTERWORD

What Must YOU Do Now?

"Be a "YES, I CAN" person in a no I can't world!" – Bruce Pulver

TedX Speaker, Author, Communication Strate

The stories, messages, and experiences shared in the preceding chapters are indeed from amazing CHANGE makers whom all started with a dream and their treasure chest of potential. Please see them through the lens of examples. They are NOT measurements of comparison for what YOU should be or do. As readers and world changers, I also urge you to take in each story and absorb the inspiration that speaks to you. Equally, please resist comparing yourself to others, but instead only to your life and what YOU will make of yours. By merely striving to get and be a little better each and every day, the positive impact you will make over your lifetime will be immeasurable. Every person is put on this earth with unique God-given, innate talents, called **GIFTS**. I call them

God | Installed | Features | To | Share

These GIFTS are wrapped in the pretty paper called potential. Shiny bows and ribbons can blind us with their bright glitter. We can too often stare at the packaging and ponder what is inside. While it is fine to admire the packaging, the real value in the GIFTS is when they are unwrapped, explored, developed, expanded, challenged, honed, and ultimately realized by sharing them. It is only by sharing that their complete value can be realized.

I challenge you to listen to your heart and your soul. Seek to understand what you hear. How it speaks to you, where it is leading you. This is called your passion. When you hear it, apply yourself to learn everything you can. I call this mantra ABL (always be learning). Then apply yourself to taking everything you learn and inject this knowledge and wisdom into your passion in a way that makes a positive impact on those around you, your family, your friends, and equally your community. This is **Passion with Purpose**. Seek not fortune and fame but to impact one person in an uplifting way.

Creating constant RIPPLES is the way to reach the greatest application of your GIFTS.

Our impact on the world manifests from our **RIPPLES**. Let them be measured not by the size of the stones we toss in the pond, but by the number of times we toss stones with only the intent of helping others.

R each into our bag of GIFTS
I nto our desire to give
P ull out a helping pebble
P itch it into the pond of need
L et the rings release and expand
E xpend no reward, REPEAT
S et your RIPPLE in motion

Let's create RIPPLES with our GIFTS. You will make your CHANGE in the world! How? You will find it easy to get excited and inspired to **COMMIT** to make the change. One way to look at the initial COMMIT is to say

Count | On | Me | Making | It | There

That is one part of the process. However, what happens when you get to the point where you don't want to anymore? Push your mindset to say I must not just commit but also commit to the commitment.

What? Yes…

"Count On Me Making It There" is merely a declaration. When the declaration fades and you want to quit, here is another way to solidify the commitment.

C ome every day with positive expectations
O wn how we use our time
M ake and keep promises to OURSELVES
M ake growth and service the priority
I nvest in actions that move us to our goals
T hen realize (with our real eyes) the outcomes

Get ready! When you want to rock the world with your change, you will face challenges and obstacles. The discouragement will be stifling. The noise will be penetrating. Please remember this message when you want to give up; it is ALWAYS too early to quit. You never know the power "one more try" has against the pressure to give in. When you are driven to be a CHANGE maker, focus on the **CHANGE** you want to make this way:

C hallenge Disruptively
H elp Endlessly
A ct Compassionately
N avigate Pragmatically
G et after it Tenaciously
E ngage Passionately

Now, Let's COMMIT to CHANGE and making your own RIPPLES. You got this!

Changing the world one story at a time

Arianna Fox
United States

Known across the region as a little ball of joy and energy, Arianna Fox is a girlpreneur, best-selling triple author, motivational speaker, actress, voiceover talent, and teen influencer. Arianna may come in a small package, but her ideas are as revolutionary as they are wide-reaching. For several years now, Arianna has devoted her life and much of her time to reaching out to others to spread messages of hope, inspiration, and self-confidence. Making a positive impact upon others and helping them rock their lives to maximum potential is part of this upcoming girlpreneur's goal for her interactions with kids, tweens, teens, adults, and all.

Changing the world
one story at a time

Riyad Maroof Hassan
India

Riyad Maroof Hassan is a 14-year-old Indian author, talk show host,
director, social entrepreneur, podcaster, poet, Global Child Rights
Ambassador, singer, content creator, and History & STEM Analyst.
He has authored two books and is the director and creator of the
first-ever historical web show developed by children - "Trouvaille".
He is the Young Program Lead of Child Development Initiatives at
MIT Square, London. He is the founder of The Clipping Universe
which comprises a media house The Clippers and a child council
The Clippers Child Council of India. He dreams of inner
development among people and developing the dream is his action.

Changing the world
one story at a time

Kellina Powell
Canada

A young entrepreneur who loves to help people with their personal growth and educate others about the deaf community. Little do people know Kellina is actually a hard of hearing person. She became deaf at the age of 4. She recently graduated with a psychology degree and is now starting her own online coaching business while launching her book.

#DeafCommunity | International Speaker | Advocate | Life Coach for Young Professionals with Disabilities creating & supporting positive mental health so they can live an inspired life.

Young Changemakers

Changing the world
one story at a time

Zackary Ford
United States

Known as an inspirational and encouraging individual, Zack is a multifaceted and unique creator. He is a multi-platform content creator, podcaster, independent Christian singer, songwriter, and musician. Zack is an aspiring author who is writing his first book, and his mission is to inspire "GenZers," teens, young adults, and adults to live their purpose and lead them to greatness! He has devoted his life to spreading kindness, positive energy, and encouraging others to be the light using their gifts and talents, by speaking their stories and sharing their message.

Changing the world one story at a time

Noor Yousef Aldalahma
Jordan

A tech freak, sports addict, and coach but most importantly a young passionate teenager that aspires to make the world a better place through technology. A silver medal winner of Genius Olympiad, a silver medal holder of English Language Olympics (Arab-region), and winner of best robot design in the Arab robotics championship are some of the awards she has won. She has worked on many projects and inventions, to name a few: a bracelet to indicate strokes and help people with dementia and Alzheimer's, a system to help blind people in universities live a normal life and be more independent, and a water filtering system using fast food leftovers. Besides her tech life, Noor is a second degree black belt holder, a basketball coach and a soccer player. Noor aims to change the lives of people and help the environment through sports and technology.

Changing the world one story at a time

Rion Cruz
United States

A dedicated and young entrepreneur who is working towards an overall goal of impacting his communities through mentorship, entrepreneurship, and coaching. He is a certified personal trainer as well, who specializes in peak performance for athletes and the general public. Rion obtained his certification through the prestigious National Academy of Sports Medicine and is currently the CEO and founder of New Realm Peak Performance. Not to mention, Rion is also a part of his family's company, Ashtree Wealth Group. His main area of focus is real estate investing and development. Ultimately, Rion is set to make his mark in the world of entrepreneurship and leadership, finding purpose in his path to help others and to carve his legacy for years to come.

Changing the world one story at a time

Sanju Kahuja
India

While being in high school, Sanju got mindful about money and self-development, so she began learning everything she could. From that moment, it became the most interesting thing, and she decided to put what she was learning into practice and got into affiliate marketing. She has trained over 2000 aspiring learners like herself to become independent. She is now on a mission to help 100,000 students become independent as well. She is an avid reader by heart, marketer by profession, and content creator by Passion. Her next move would be to connect with like-minded, intellectually accomplished people and build something impactful together to add value in other people's lives. Whatever she can do to contribute to society to make a more positive impact she will do; as well, she will never stop learning!

Changing the world one story at a time

Manasi Patil
India

A 16-year-old from Mumbai, who believes her dreams make her. She believes in the potential of youth, as well as changemaking through actions, and has been striding down the path for a couple of years now. A published author at 14, Manasi loves all things books, poetry, and literature. She believes communication is a key to creating a change and is working on spreading the message to 'reinforce the GenZ potential' throughout the GenZ community, be it through her TEDx talk, views shared at events and conferences, or the workshops she conducts in schools and organizations. With a keen interest in STEM, Manasi has also been a space-science columnist at RobinAge, where her articles were read by students all over India. With her "crazy" dreams and visions, Manasi is here to make a difference by impacting other youth like herself.

Changing the world one story at a time

Anagha Rajesh
UAE/India

A storyteller, community builder and undergrad researcher - that is Anagha Rajesh in a nutshell. She is from India and was raised in the UAE. She is the founder and CEO of Yours Mindfully, a youth-led organization on a mission to make mental health resources accessible to 1 million young people by 2030. Anagha leads a diverse team who has managed to impact 10,000+ young people over the last 3 years. Anagha has been placed among the top 10 finalists for the Global Student Prize 2022 and is an Ashoka Young Changemaker. She loves reading, Indian classical dance, traveling and all flavors of ice-cream. She is passionate about the intersection of STEM, public policy and entrepreneurship and hopes to pursue a career in that space.

Changing the world
one story at a time

Siddhita Mohanty
India

Founder of Bloom Riddhi Siddhi. She is also a 13-year-old Digital Entrepreneur, Visual Graphic Designer, Innovator, Certified Android app and game developer, Creative digital 3D designer, and Certified Junior robot developer. Her vision is to emerge as a Global Leader to serve for the well-being of the society. Her mission is to serve people for the betterment of their mental health as a World Class Medical Scientist with a specialization in Neuroscience. Her hobbies are Graphic Design, Coding, Creative Writing, Solving Puzzles, Playing Badminton and Cricket. She has created 1000+ 3D designs and 50+ apps.

Changing the world one story at a time

Sarah Syed
Canada

After witnessing the detrimental impacts the climate crisis has on communities around the world when she was 9 years old, Sarah has made it her goal to not only advocate for a sustainable future but find tangible, actionable solutions. She has worked on biodegradable plastic made from food scraps to combat single-use plastics. Her interest in emerging technology has led Sarah to work on using common fruit peels to design a biosorbent with polysaccharide aerogel that can remove oil, heavy metals, and organic compounds from water. Sarah's work has been recognized by MP Dan Albas, NDP Critic for Environment and Climate Change Laurel Collins, the Lieutenant Governor of Ontario, The Weather Network, Toronto Star, and Diversity in Action Magazine. She has also been named a Top 25 Under 25 Environmentalist in Canada, Ontario Junior Citizen, National Nature Inspirational Youth, Top 20 Youth globally, and has many more achievements to her name at just 17!

Changing the world one story at a time

Liza Magaña
El Salvador

A 14-year-old, Christian singer and youth leader. She is taking advantage of technology to help other youth find their confidence and believe in themselves through the teachings of Jesus. Liza hosts a group where she, along with other teens and tweens from Latin America and the United States, get to know more about God through the scriptures. She is a very enthusiastic young leader and her passion is to help others know more about what faith in Jesus really is.

Young Changemakers

Changing the world one story at a time

Bruce Pulver
abovethechatterourwordsmatter.com

A Keynote and TEDx Speaker, Published Author, and "WORD"shop leader. Bruce is an authority on the *Power of Our Words* in driving our Outcomes. His book, "Above The Chatter, Our Words Matter," teaches and activates how our words, change our mindset, and drive our outcomes to create greater success. Bruce often supports his clients with workshops and in-service education programs and with every speaking engagement donates books to organizations serving others in need including hospitals, shelters, support groups, and more.

Young Changemakers

Changing the world
one story at a time

Glenn Marsden
imperfectlyperfectcampaign.org

Founder of the Imperfectly Perfect Campaign, who has spent the last 4 years bringing awareness to mental health by building relationships with public figures and showing the human side, that most people don't see. His mission with the campaign is to educate, support, advocate and provide public awareness so that the conversation around mental health disorders normalizes, enabling our children, grandchildren and future generations to live without stigmas attached to mental health.

Young Changemakers

Changing the world one story at a time

Evan Carmichael
believe.evancarmichael.com

An entrepreneur who BELIEVES in entrepreneurs. Evan has great success inspiring others through his content. His YouTube channel for entrepreneurs has over 3 million subscribers and 500 million views. He has written 4 books and speaks globally. He wants to solve the world's biggest problem, people don't #Believe in themselves enough. Forbes named him one of the world's top 40 social marketing talents and Inc. named him one of the 100 great leadership speakers and 25 social media keynote speakers you need to know. Evan owns Canada's largest salsa dance studio and has a giant Doritos bag in front of him all day long to remind him that he's stronger than the Doritos. Toronto is his home. He's a husband, father, League of Legends Fan and Teemo main.

Changing the world one story at a time

Naveen Jain
naveenjain.com

An intensely curious entrepreneur and philanthropist, Naveen Jain focuses on ideas that push humanity forward. Driven to solve the world's biggest problems and propelled by his imagination, Naveen pushes big dreams into action, spurring massive cultural and technological change. With an audacious vision, he knows no limits. His moonshot vision breaks through barriers; his magnetic personality inspires the impossible. He is the author of the award-winning book, Moonshots: Creating a World of Abundance. From local boy to lunar visionary, Naveen sees beyond the current business and technological landscape, creating companies that make a true impact. As the founder of Viome, Moon Express, World Innovation Institute, TalentWise, Intelius, and Infospace, Naveen is focused on audacious ideas that will positively impact billions of people.

Young Changemakers

Changing the world one story at a time

Kristi Maggio
kristimaggio.com

Entrepreneur in education, youth mentor and author of the award-winning book, "Follows and Likes Is This All That I'm Worth?" Kristi is dedicated to creating access to education and employment opportunities worldwide. For over 20 years, she watched many children fail and feel inadequate merely because they didn't fit into the traditional way of learning. She chose to take action and founded a school that gives students the tools to create success in their life no matter who they are or where they come from. After starting Maggio Multicultural Academy in 2016, Kristi's mission became clear, to impact the lives of 1 billion youth in the next 10 years by providing an educational program based on entrepreneurship and applied learning. It has become Kristi's obsession, to make a new ecosystem that provides youth with the skills they need before graduating high school, as well as diminish generational poverty.

OTHER BOOKS BY THE AUTHORS

Kristi Maggio	Follows and Likes Is This All That I'm Worth?
Naveen Jain	Moonshots Creating a World of Abundance
Evan Carmichael	Your One Word Built To Serve Momentum
Bruce Pulver	Above the Chatter, Our Words Matter
Arianna Fox	Sabre Black False Awakening
Manasi Patil	Why Ignore Them? Let's Confront & Win! The Cousins' Crime
Kellina Powell	Everyday I Am Just Deaf!

www.ingramcontent.com/pod-product-compliance
Lightning Source LLC
Chambersburg PA
CBHW060522130626
46553CB00002B/608